Case Studies

for

MARKETING

Students

Prof. Kisholoy Roy

Table of Contents

PREFACE

This book is a compilation of case studies focusing on four fundamental areas of marketing viz. brand management, services marketing, retail marketing and sales management. The book is classified into four sections based on the above areas. Every care has been taken by the author to see to it that each section has case studies that contribute to the holistic understanding of a subject area.

Conceptual understanding of the subject area along with application of theory is what this book offers. The questions at the end of each case study test the understanding of a case study by a student. The author hopes that this book will serve good to all students pursuing marketing management curriculum in various Indian universities as well as in various global institutions.

SECTION – I

CASE Studies on Brand MANAGEMENT

THE Health Drink WAR

Health drinks are a part of the functional food and drinks category which also includes such beverages as energy foods and drinks, sports drinks, health soft drinks, etc. The category of health drinks also includes such drinks as soy milk and other soy based drinks, fruit juices, targeted health drinks, such as calcium rich drinks for the bones, and any other new age drink with health benefit such as many herb and berries that are coming into the international markets from Asia and South America. Over a dozen health drinks promising weight loss, cell-damage-reducing antioxidants and natural energy have reached supermarket shelves in 2007, while many more still in the pipeline.

The total sales of health foods and health drinks in 2006 were approximately $20 billion through distribution channels such as mass-market, television shopping channels, health/natural food stores, large discounter houses such as Wal-Mart, and warehouse "big-box" clubs. With more functional foods and beverages available in the market combined with medically beneficial ingredients, health and wellness are now included in top criteria driving consumer food choices.

The health drinks market is growing rapidly but is still a small industry in the U.S. This is generally grouped with the category of beverages or the sub category of sports drinks or energy drinks. The pure health drinks market is currently just a fraction of those categories by most industry definitions.

In 2005 global sales of "healthy" drinks, including bottled water, fruit juices, and sports and energy drinks may have been as high as $138 billion, which would represent 45% of the entire soft-drinks market. Growth rates in specific categories of this industry may be seven times higher than those for carbonated drinks for example. And the sector continues to gain market share as consumers move away from alternative soft drinks towards health drinks.

Now come to the Indian market Scenario. In Indian market there are two main market's player- Horlicks & Complan. The health drink from GSK (GlaxoSmithKline), Horlicks, has been traditionally targeted at elders and positioned as a 'great family nourisher'. However, in early 2000s, the communication was changed to 'pleasurable family nourisher' with the introduction of different flavors such as chocolate, vanilla and elaichi. The TV commercial had children going around the town, cheering Epang Opang Jhapang – a chant without any meaning. However, the TVC showed their mothers deciding on the choice of health drink. Horlicks' competitor, Complan, promised to make the kids taller. Shorter kids' friends coaxed them to request their mothers to give them Complan. Now, Horlicks has gone a step further in promising not only height, but a stronger body and a sharper mind. Horlicks wants the children to decide on their health drink. The new campaign for Horlicks gives the kids a motto: 'Badlo Apne Bachpan ka Size'.

Horlicks is the leading health food drink in India and as the "Most trusted Drink Brand" (economic Times suevey, 2004).In India it enjoys more than half of the health food drink market. Although it has been a popular brand in the Indian market since 1930s, Horlicks underwent a revamp in 2003 to further increase its relevance. The modern & contemporary Horlicks offers 'pleasurable nourishments' with a delicious range of flavors including vanilla, toffee, elaichi and chocolate. In India Horlicks available has been scientifically developed and it specifically caters to the nutritional needs of Indian children. It helps meet the requirements of essential nutrients in children, such as, iron and vitamins, these nutrients are very important for school going children for their attention , concentration and memory as well as their physical performance and growth. Horlicks has established this through a large clinical trial among school going children.

Horlicks holds 58% the Rs.1.900 crore health drinks market and is currently a Rs. 1, 000 crore brands in India. From 1930 to till date Horlicks leads it superiority in the market by positioning & repositioning strategy. For a short while, Horlicks has also come up with a packaging innovation in which the Horlicks bottle will be place inside a graphical can to attract attention at retail stores. From a drink that was supposed to promote a good night's sleep to one that can that can help children grow taller, stronger & sharper .Now, its brand image too has changed – from a boring health drink recommended by doctors to something that is nourishing and enjoyable.

In 1992, as its market share grew, the brand extended itself to a new product – Horlicks Biscuits. In 1994, it started singing the 'micro nutrient' story, followed by its 'smart nutrients 'campaigns in 1998. The brand underwent a massive transformation in 2003, when almost everything about it changed – from the taste and flavor to the packaging. It also changed its positioning. It was nourishing, yes but also tasty. For children in 2005 Horlicks was launched junior Horlicks. The company recently re-launched Horlicks in three new variants – vanilla, honey & chocolate - apart from the regular malt. The new Horlicks composition is also accompanied by contemporary packaging in hues of bright blue & orange. In 2009 Horlicks launched a nutrition bar and in the year2010, Horlicks launched noodles with the brand name – Foodles.

Complan was first developed by Glaxo in the 1950s as a powered food for use in the hospitals. When reconstituted with water it provided all essential nutrients and could be fed to patients through a tube as well as mouth. Its name derived from complete planned nutrition. Today Complan is focused on providing nutrition products suitable for all members of the family, through three core products, Complan (balanced nutrition for family), Casilan (for sportsman) & Complanshake (to tackle clinical malnutrition).Complan is available in various form like for family, for seniors and also for weight management. There also have two varieties in Casilan one for sportsman and another Casilan for health. Complanshake is available in a variety of delicious flavors like original, vanilla, chocolate, strawberry and banana. The brand Complan has also extended to biscuits.

A TVC for Horlicks in 2010 has Darsheel Safary (of Taare Jameen Par fame).The TVC is supported by print , radio and on-ground activities and extended to Horlicks school program , whiz kids contest. Lately, a comparative advertising strategy has been adopted by Horlicks which claims that children grow taller, stronger and sharper by consuming Horlicks.

Questions

1. Describe the brand anatomy of Horlicks & Complan.
2. Describe the levels of two brands – Horlicks & Complan.
3. Make a comparative analysis of brand identity prism for Horlicks & Complan.
4. Describe the line extension and brand extension of Horlicks & Complan mentioned in the case study.
5. Describe positioning and repositioning strategy of Horlicks.
6. Does the contents & execution of comparative advertising mentioned in the case study stick to ethical branding practices? Explain with adequate reasoning.

ADVERTISING Campaign of Tata SALT

The 'Maine desh ka namak khaya hai' TATA advertisement campaign in 2002 offered viewers an instant connection. In India, salt and loyalty have been associated from time immemorial. 'Namak halal" and "Namak Haram" are commonly used terms for honest and dishonest people respectively. According to cultural connotations, after consuming salt at a person's house the one who has consumed the salt should not cheat his/her host. The campaign connected with the consumer at an emotional level.

TATA Chemicals Ltd (TCL) started manufacturing salt in 1939 after establishing a solar salt works at Mithapur, Gujarat. It pioneered the concept of iodized and vacuum-evaporated salt in India in the early 1980s and created a need that was not felt by consumers before. Interestingly, the opportunity came accidentally, when in 1983, the company needed fresh water for its boilers that produced soda ash at its Mithapur plant in Gujarat. As fresh water was scarce in the area, the company began processing sea water. Salt of high quality was the by-product. Estimated to be worth Rs.10 billion, TATA has a 21% share in the packaged iodized salt industry in India. According to A.C. Neilson in Brand Track 2002-03, 90% of the people surveyed across the country had tried TATA salt at least once. The salt market is pegged at five million tones out of which 1.5 million tones are of the branded variety. TATA salt leads the market with a 40% share. According to analysts, TATA was able to get the leadership position in the category as it had the first mover advantage. Some competing brands include Annapurna from HLL, Dandi from Kumwar Ajay industries, Shudh from the Mirma Group, Captain Cook from DCW Home foods, Ashiwaad from the ITC stable, besides some international brand likeCargil and Congra. From 'vacuum-evaporated' to 'iodized' from 'free flow' to 'danedar', one does not see much brand differential among competitive brands, hence the need for a strong and memorable advertising plank and better packaging. One finds vigorous advertising by major players in the mass media. Looking at the overseas potential, TATA, according to industry buzz, is exploring the Middle East market and those of neighboring countries like Nepal and Bangladesh.

Tetley's overseas distribution network could come in handy for marketing the salt in these countries. In order to expand the user base, TATA salt that is priced at Rs 8 per kilogram, against un-branded salts at Rs 3-4 per kg. The company has launched its economy brand 'Samundar' at Rs 5 per kg. Purity, trust, and value have been the planks of its communication strategy. The earlier catch-line, 'Namak ho TATA ka, TATA namak', when more competitors came into the market, and the need for an emotional bond was felt. Besides an aggressive approach to branding, the company improved packaging, sales, and supply chain management. According to company sources, consumer research by TATA Chemicals in June 2002 revealed that people had a sense of insecurity and a disgust for corruption, which they thought were eroding Indian democracy. The insights that the research provided helped in tapping patriotic and nationalist favor. TATA took the opportunity to be associated with the universal theme of 'remaining ture to one's salt and to one's country'. This was the philosophy behind the 'Meine desh ka namak khaya hai' tagline.

The new packaging, with the visual of delectable cuisine, backed this. 'Vacuum evaporated' and 'iodized' were clearly written on the pack a plank that other competitors also used. The advertisement with the visual of a banana leaf and a pinch of salt in a corner (a traditional serving in south India) with the headline (figure 1.12): 'To Indian housewives, our salt always comes first' and the catch line 'Meine desh ka namak khaya hai' was considered by analysts as amongst the greatest advertisements when it appeared. In order to connect with communities, TATA salt has used public relations to sustain the brand on a ling term basis. Since the launch of the 'Desh ka namak' campaign in 2002, during some specified months, a small percentage of money that accrues from the sale of TATA salt is set aside for economically disadvantaged children. In the two years since the launch, 25,000 children have been provided with one year of education.

Questions

1. Salt is a generic product and is basic to human existence. Why then in your view, is there so much competition and rigorous marketing in this category?
2. Who are the major players in the branched salt category and what are their advertising planks?
3. Comment on the 'branding through patriotism' route adopted by Tata Salt.

BRANDING Through Controversies: The Benetton WAY!

Controversial advertising has been on the rise for quite some time. Some of the factors triggering the phenomenon include growing complexity of the society, increased awareness of side-effects of various products and enhance attempt of ad agencies to become more creative in order to gain more attention and awareness of target audience. It was this motive that stimulated Benetton to come up with creative outputs for its brand of apparels and accessories which were termed as Shock advertising and controversial by the world for the advertisements defied the norms set by the society.

Benetton Group has been engaged in the manufacturing and distribution of clothing, undergarments, shoes, cosmetics and accessories. Benetton also licensed its brand name for a number of products like sunglasses, stationery, cosmetics, linens, watches, toys, steering wheels and knobs for automobile gearshifts, golf equipments, designer condoms, luggage and designer pagers, etc. The group's principal brands included United Colors of Benetton (UCB), Sisley, PlayLife, Nordica, Prince, Rollerblade, and Killer Loop.

Benetton is one of the strongest brands in the world which is well-known for its unusual advertising techniques and themes, most of them bordering on controversy and debate. From the 1989 debut of "Breastfeeding" and "Handcuffs" and continuing through to the present with 2003's "Food for Life", the startling images were Benetton's key platform in the careful campaign to build its mark, UNITED COLORS OF BENETTON. Benetton utilized "shock value" and the reality of photographs to grab viewer's attention and to make their brand name memorable. Unlike most advertisements which centered on a company's product or image, Benetton's advertising campaigns addressed social and political issues like racial integration, AIDS awareness, war, poverty, child labor, death, pollution etc. The company tried more to "communicate" to the world about these issues rather than to "sell" apparel and accessories.

Benetton's long journey toward its destiny as a non-follower of stereotypes began with its ad campaigns in mid 1980s. Happy groups of multiracial kids were replaced by "couples" representing an all-new interpretation of difference. In this cycle, the word "different" became a close cousin of "controversial." Benetton learned that dealing with the issue of difference within the process of advertising is not an easy task. Often, an attempt to bring different individuals together can lead to conflict instead of happiness and euphoria. Many ads from the period were an expression of this process. One represented religious and political conflict (the Palestinian and the Israeli).

Another depicted religious and sexual conflict (a priest kissing a nun), and yet another portrayed moral conflict (the stereotypes of good and evil, symbolized by an angel and the devil).All of these conflicts were based on taboos, on the impossibility of co-existence, on a difference that separates rather than unites. By acknowledging these differences and prohibitions, the brand appeared more involved. It took sides, rather than presenting a simple "objective" portrayal of the world; it made a commitment to foster the cohabitation of opposites, to break down barriers and ensure dialogue. Benetton had a plan: to integrate opposites, to unite differences under a single flag, the flag of its own logo. In this phase, the "product" gradually disappeared from the advertisements. Traditional advertising messages made the product their obvious focus, so that the campaign would have a measurable commercial impact. Benetton took another path, wagering that once the brand's identity had been established, the product would become one of its attributes. The company was now taking hold on all the continents. Paradoxically, the growing popularity and availability of tangible Benetton merchandise—the goods people could buy in more than 5,000 stores worldwide—translated into the disappearance of those goods from its ads.

In 1988, the company started mixing culture and legends. New advertisements featured Adam and Eve, Joan of Arc and Marilyn Monroe, Leonardo de Vinci and Julius Caesar, all captioned with the slogan: "United Superstars of Benetton."." Similar campaigns featured animals- a wolf and a lamb with the tagline: "United Friends of Benetton."

In 1989, Benetton decided to cancel its agreement with outside advertising agencies and develop campaigns in house. With less than ten people managing the entire process, Benetton could produce advertisements, at about one-third the cost of its competitors. Famous advertisements during the late 1980s included a black hand and a white hand linked by a handcuff and a black woman breast-feeding a white baby. The black woman- white baby advertisement was severely criticized by many who thought that Benetton was reminding blacks of the days of slavery when black women breast-fed white babies. However, Benetton maintained that such photos symbolized universal brotherhood.

In 1991, Benetton introduced a number of advertisements that discussed other social issues. The advertisements were a means to draw attention to important social problems and thereby generate public discussion. Throughout the early 1990s, Benetton advertisements featured a cemetery (signifying war deaths), many different brightly colored condoms, a baby with an umbilical cord, a priest and a nun kissing, etc. The advertisement featuring the priest and nun seriously offended the Pope of Vatican and the religious sentiments of many. The image of the baby with an umbilical cord invited mixed responses. In the company's view, advertisement simply conveyed the beauty of new life. More specifically the advertisement was to convey the universal idea of love as a force from which life itself is born and that a baby symbolizes the most permanent form of love. The photo set off a huge controversy throughout Europe and many wanted it to be banned. At the same time, however, the image was exhibited in a Flemish museum as part of a show celebrating the images of motherhood.

In 1992, Benetton released advertisements that had a political flavor. A series of photojournalistic images concerning the AIDS crisis, environmental disaster, political violence, war exile, etc. were shortlisted for developing ads on the above said themes. These appeared in various journals and magazines as well as on billboards without written text except for the conspicuous insertion of the green and white Benetton logo located in the margins.

Though most of its advertisements were severely rebuked by governments, media and general public alike, Benetton was found to go one step further by adopting "reality advertising." Advertisements included: A dying AIDS victim with his family at his bedside, an African guerrilla holding a Kalachnikov and a human leg bone, a boat overcrowded with Albanians, a group of African refugees, and a car in flames after a Mafia bombing, a family weeping before the bloodied corpse of a Mafioso, two Indians caught in a flood in Calcutta, etc. Benetton also launched an advertisement with a series of masculine and feminine genitals, all different ages, and all different colors with the label "United Colors of Benetton." A more shocking advertisement showed close-ups of various parts of the human body (pubis, arms, stomach, and bottom) tattooed with the English abbreviation "HIV Positive." The tattoo mark was similar to the numbers tattooed by Nazis on concentration camp prisoners. Benetton advertisements also promoted homosexuality: Two smiling men cheek to cheek, two women—one white and the other black, holding an Asian baby, wrapped in the same blanket, etc.

Other controversial advertisements included a black stallion mounting a white mare, three identical human hearts, with stickers announcing different ethnic groups "white, black and yellow." The hearts portrayed that everybody was the same in the inside, no matter what the outside skin color was.

Apart from advertisements for billboards and magazines, Benetton also created a number of catalogs titled "People and Places." Catalog themes included Young People in Tokyo, Sunflowers (featuring children with Down's syndrome), Jerusalem, Ponzano (Italy), Corleone (Italy), China, India, etc. These catalogs featured pictures of people from the above-mentioned countries. In 1998, Benetton used images of Arabs and Jews living and working together in Israel. Titled "Enemies," the cover showed a kiss between a 24-year-old Israeli student and her 22-year-old Bedouin boyfriend. The catalo included photos of an Arab grocer and a Jewish customer, Jewish and Arab youth leaders, a mixed kindergarten of Jewish and Arab kids, a music band comprising of Jews and Arabs, etc

In the US, the company opened the campaign with a 96-page supplement that was attached to the February issue of Talk magazine. Entitled "We, On Death Row", it featured photographs of 26 condemned men in different US states. The written profiles were mostly sympathetic, focusing on the regrets expressed by the men about their plights and offering almost no details of the crimes they were convicted of committing.

Benetton faced several stiff oppositions for challenging the existing norms through its commercials. Most painful of all, however, was a decision by Sears Roebuck, the retail monolith based in Chicago, to tear up a franchising contract that it had only just reached with Benetton, purely because of the advertising campaign. In February, Sears dropped Benetton and cleared from its shelves all of the Benetton-labelled clothes that it had started to manufacture and to sell under the franchise agreement.

In 1995, government authorities in Germany banned Benetton advertisements featuring child laborers, the human body stamped "HIV Positive," and a bird stuck in an oil slick. They were banned because these advertisements exploited suffering. The newborn advertisement was withdrawn from the media in Italy, France and UK. The more the company's advertisements were banned, the more Benetton got publicity. Benetton was also sued by many of its retail outlets that believed the provocative advertisements drove away customers. Many retailers criticized Benetton's strategy. The strong force behind Benetton's advertisements was Oliviero Toscani who created advertisements the less traditional way. Toscani's responsibility, as Benetton's creative director, was to document social realities rather than promote sales. His advertising style was in strict contrast to most advertising styles and he identified a number of drawbacks in traditional advertising. He believes that the industry as a whole should change the way advertisements are used. The reason being that consumer-spending pattern had changed over the years. Following the controversy surrounding the death row campaign, Oliviero Toscani quit Benetton in May 2000.

Benetton realized that it had crossed even the boundaries of unconventional advertising with the death-row campaign. Various surveys suggested that loyal customers also decided against shopping at Benetton. Following Toscani's exit, Benetton highlighted its advertising strategy for the future. Benetton, however, maintained that the company would still maintain its "socially responsible" image by working on non-controversial causes like racial discrimination, poverty, child labor, AIDS awareness, etc. Since 2001, the brand has alternated, every three seasons, conventional product campaigns with increasingly wide-ranging institutional campaigns.

In 2003, a Benetton communication campaign, a book and a COLORS supplement in collaboration with the World Food Program, a front-line UN agency in the fight against world famine. The campaign highlighted the problem of hunger, which is still the greatest humanitarian emergency around the world even though it has, to all intents and purposes, been forgotten by the media and the general public. The aim was to show how food can be a catalyst for social change, a major engine for peace and development that can radically change an individual's future prospects of life.

In 2008, a global communication campaign in favor of micro-credit in Senegal was released by Benetton. . Benetton highlighted on entrepreneurial spirit of African continent. It has been thus observed that over the years, Benetton has come up with socially relevant advertisements but then they were termed controversial and outrageous probably because the way they were executed or because of their content. However, Benetton's brand building tactics revolves around controversial advertisements which many feel have on one hand invited wrath from many quarters but on the other have contributed to the high awareness, recognition and resonance for the brand.

Questions

1. Describe some of the controversial advertisements launched by Benetton in the 1980s?
2. Do you think controversial advertisements can contribute to a brand's resonance?
3. Create a brand identity prism of Benetton.
4. 'It is the Shock advertisements and not the traditional advertisements that can impart sustainability to Brand Benetton.' Debate.

EXPANDING Brand Scope: The Sugar Free CASE

In marketing theory, there are different ways to reposition and grow a brand. One among them is to expand the usage situations and finding new uses for the brand and through new variants. Sugar Free Natura, the sugar substitute brand from Zydus has been slowly and consistently expanding the scope of the brand on similar lines.

Sugar Free launched itself as a sugar substitute for beverages. So instead of using sugar in beverages like tea, coffee, cool drinks etc, the brand tried to position itself as a healthy sugar substitute. Rather than specifically focusing on diabetic patients (who obviously needs such a product), Sugar Free concentrated on a larger consumer base by positioning itself as healthy alternative to sugar.

But the brand realized that focusing just on beverages severely limits the usage of the product. Hence the brand launched a campaign expanding the usage of the brand by telling the consumers to use Sugar Free not only for beverages but also for all other delicacies which require sugar like home made sweets. The brand roped in popular Chef Sanjeev Kapoor as the brand ambassador for the purpose who was found advocating the use of Sugar Free Natura in place of sugar in common Indian desserts in the brand communication.

In due course of time, the brand moved into the next level of value addition by launching flavor sachets for tea. Two new flavors of Sugar Free Natura viz. Ginger Masala and Lemon Mint were launched. The variants of the brand gave many customers double the reason to buy the brand.

There has been a further repositioning of Sugar Free lately. The new campaign for the brand takes a slight variation in the positioning from health to fitness. While both health and fitness are in the same level, fitness platform is more appealing to a broader set of younger consumers than health. Health is defensive while fitness is proactive.

Another interesting factor is that the new campaign tends to associate the unique shape of the Sugar Free with body shape. Many feel that it's a smart move by the ad agency to link the shape of the bottle and a perfect body shape.

Sugar Free Gold, a variant of the Sugar Free brand has been found to run aggressive campaigns by roping in two celebrities for two different markets in India. The brand is being endorsed by Simran (Tamil actress) in the South while Bollywood actress Bipasha Basu endorses the brand in the North. The campaigns are based on the fitness platform. *"fitness ke baare me hum bahut sochtey hain"* – We think a lot about fitness – the diet that goes for a toss at the first sign of laddu, that morning walk that is sacrificed for more sleep… So, why not take that first step – read, short cut – to fitness by switching to Sugar Free Gold? I like, I like – good advertising based on solid consumer insights.

Sugar Free is a brand that has realized the potential for a healthy alternative to sugar. India has an exploding diabetic population and such a product hold tremendous scope in future. The only factor that limits the growth of Sugar Free is the higher price. The price severely limits the repeat purchase and regular use of this product. The category will grow only if the brand is able to break the price barrier.

Questions

1. Comment on the way Zydus has expanded the scope of its brand Sugar Free?
2. Opine on the extension strategies adopted for Sugar Free?

3. Zydus has gone for celebrity endorsements for a product like Sugar Free. Is this recommendable? Explain with adequate reasoning.

THE Axe EFFECT!

Axe as a brand was born in France in the Year 1983. As on 2010, the brand is Unilever's best selling brand worldwide.

Axe deodorant was launched in India during 1999. The brand launch was very quiet and theoretically the brand was having the strategy of Slow skimming i.e. High Price Low Promotion. Axe at that time was the leading men's deodorant brand in Europe and was popular in India in the Grey market (available in duty paid shops). HLL may have launched this brand inspired by the volume of Axe sold in the Grey market. At that time, the deodorant market was a nascent one with an estimated market size of Rs 72 crore. HUL had the brands Denim and Rexona and was ruling the market. Axe was priced at a premium above the Denim brand which was positioned as a male deodorant brand. Axe initially was launched in the fragrance Java, Alaska and Atlantic. HUL did not bother to fine tune its Promotional mix to Indian market but just imported the promotions which means that the company just ran the ads which was popular in the Europe and other foreign markets.

In 2002, Axe had a market share of over 35% which made HUL (then HLL) phase out Denim brand to concentrate on Axe. Axe has been the 'naughtiest' brand in the Indian market. The brand is targeted at male aged 16-25 years. Internationally this brand targets male aged 15-25. The brand targets all 'Young at heart" naughty guys. The brand has its brand values of Cool, Fashionable and Stylish. The biggest strength of this brand is the underlying message or the DNA which is that the brand users are high on Confidence and always for the Axe users, Girls Makes the First Move. Branding experts feel that the biggest competitive advantage of this brand is its complete monopoly over this brand proposition. All its campaigns revolve round this central theme of Seduction where Girl makes the first move.

All the advertisements for the brand have significant subliminal implications. The brand assumes that Men want (Likes) to be seduced. There have been lots of ads where girls are seen drooling over Hunks in Motorcycle or in readymades, or even in Innerwear, but in most of the Axe ads, there are no Hunks, only very ordinary or even skinny kind of people getting assaulted by beautiful girls. That has made the brand more approachable. Branding experts opine that the males seen in Axe commercials are not Losers and the ads are careful to show them as confident (in one way or other) or a better term will be self assured. That is ultimate execution. The power of this Big Idea has ensured that Indian consumers lap up the foreign commercials without any hitch.

Apart from innovative communications, the brand also ensured that customers are constantly engaged with new fragrances and campaigns. In 2005, Axe had a high profile launch of its new fragrance CLICK and before that there was Axe Land campaign followed by Axe-Academy then Axe Voodoo and Axe Phenomenon.

Axe as a brand has been found to embrace the Internet to a great extent. The brand has been found to initiate its Internet based marketing initiative in India with Axe Land which involved a virtual trip to the Axe world. Globally also this brand has lot of online initiatives which are almost always naughty.

Not only the brand uses TVC's to its advantage, the print ads of Axe won several accolades in various ad events. Many cite Axe as a classic example of 360 degree branding effort. Now Axe has a common message in over 70 countries where Unilever sells this brand.

One of the reports termed the marketing strategy of Axe as "Adventurous Marketing", which is true since it's risky for a brand to deal with issues like sex and seduction.

Brand analysts feel that Axe has got every thing perfect for its success. It got its segments correct, the targeting was exemplary and so was its positioning. It has an iconic status in whichever market it has entered. It is also one of the rare brands which can boast of replicating its entire marketing mix across geographical boundaries.

Questions
1. Although Unilever standardized its promotion strategy for Axe, it clicked across markets. Cite various reasons for the same.
2. What do you mean by the term '360 degree branding effort'? Explain.
3. Present a brand identity prism of Axe?

LIRIL: A Case of Lost Brand IMAGERY

Liril as a brand of bathing soap was launched in the year 1975. Soon the brand's communication was found to capture the imagination of the nation. The advertisement featuring a girl in a bikini bathing under the waterfall with was reportedly a run away success and the Liril girl became the talk of the town. The brand was found to be consistent with its communication and effectively used the element of brand imagery. Looking back at the advertisement, many feel that it was the creativity of ad man Alyque Padamsee that did the magic for the brand. In his book, a Double Life, Padamsee mentions, *"The name Liril had been registered by Hindustan Lever from a list sent to them by Unilever in London. Levers were very keen that the soap have striations, wiggly stripes of different colours running across the tablet. I recommended the tablet be blue - because waterfall is blue with white striations. Hindustan Lever was very excited and produced 1,000 tablets for testing. At this point Derk Wooller, the Marketing Controller of Hindustan Lever's soaps division, stepped in and suggested we add the freshness of lime to our story. He felt that though the waterfall had tremendous emotional appeal, Liril needed a rational ingredient to clinch the deal. I was not averse to this but suggested that we do an `As marketed' test: Blue Liril versus Green Liril with limes. I was wrong and Wooller was right. The rest is history."*

Liril was positioned on the freshness platform right from its inception. The girl and the waterfall with the unique jingle ensured that the freshness was experienced by the audience. Liril was promoted as an experiential brand and the communication perfectly supported that.

Liril did not change its positioning for 25 years although the faces for the brand changed, the brand communication was consistent. For a certain period of time during the late 1990s, film actress Priety Zinta was found to endorse the brand. Liril was a promoted as a brand for bathing but then the communications were almost silent about the freshness aspect connected with the brand.

Since early 2000s, Liril experienced declining market share which many feel happened as the brand failed to understand the changing consumer expectations. A number of bathing soaps emerged in the Indian markets since early 1990s and there were many among them that were referred to as the bathing soap containing lime. Brand experts opine that Liril should have hold on its positioning of ' freshness " plank not by changing its communication but by communicating more, developing variants, bringing in flanking brands or variants and thus owning the whole segment for itself.

Liril introduced the Icy mint variant very late and that too with a different jingle and imagery and then the Orange Liril was launched which did not find many takers in the market. Then came the new campaign involving a couple and a new jingle " La-ira -ela". The ad was quite sensual but then the initial positioning of freshness was no where in the commercial.

Many feel that if Liril as a brand is to survive it will if it goes back to the basics. It needs to recreate the magic it created in the 1970s and that has to happen based on the freshness aspect. Brand imagery should not just be triggering nostalgia among the customers but should ideally reignite the love, passion and faith for the brand. The brand's communication should make customers go Laaaaa lalalala laaa ....

Questions

1. Explain the term brand imagery with adequate examples apart from the one mentioned in the case study?
2. Describe the 'big idea' behind the promotion of Liril in the 1970s?
3. As a brand manager, offer a suitable solution to revive the Liril brand in terms of brand resonance?

NICHE Branding Strategy of Anne FRENCH

Anne French is a niche brand. The brand is a major player in the INR 50 crore hair remover cream market in India. The brand owned by the pharmaceutical major Wyeth is now facing the heat of competition.

The Indian hair remover cream market is small because of the fact that hair removal is a touchy subject for women and this product category is seldom discussed across media. The campaigns are usually low key and brands gain popularity more through word of mouth and highly targeted advertising.

Anne French is a Depilatory cream. Depilatory creams remove hair at skin line. These creams use alkaline chemical (Calcium thioglycolate) which dissolves the protein structure of hair and causes it to separate from skin. Although there are different methods of removing unwanted hair like plucking, tweezing, threading, waxing bleaching, shaving etc, depilatory creams have gained popularity in Indian market owing to the convenience and ease of use. The only drawback is that it may cause allergy in some cases.

The product category of hair remover cream was in a stagnant stage till 2004 when Reckitt launched the global depilatory cream major Veet in the Indian market. The brand was found to cause a stir in the Indian market. Veet used Bollywood actress Katrina Kaif to endorse the brand.

The entry of Veet threatened the leadership position of Anne French. In terms of acceptability, Veet had the advantage of its global image which was further enhanced by the celebrity endorsement. Veet also tried to innovate by launching the product in a tube form. The strategy reportedly forced Anne French to launch its own tube package and also increase ad spends.

In 2007, Anne French launched the Squeeze tube and two perfume variants to counter the threat from the global leader Veet. Anne French has been found to add more value to its product by adding moisturizer and vitamin. Anne French has been trying to position itself as the product that offers smooth and silky skin in the easiest manner. Some of the latest advertisements of Anne French have been found to focus on promoting the tube variant. Although Anne French has been leading in the Indian market, its position is under threat due to a global brand. Many feel that the marketing war between the two brands can lift up the category into a high growth path. Already Anne French has taken the threat head on. It needs to be seen how Anne French defends its leadership position in the long run.

Questions

1. Comment on Anne French's strategy to counter Veet's threat in India?
2. Do you feel that celebrity endorsement will help Anne French to further protect its position vis-à-vis Veet? Explain.

BABA Ramdev: The Making of a Maverick BRAND

Baba Ramdev, a celibate since childhood, is well versed in Sanskrit Grammar, Ayurved and Vedic Philosophy. A strong Proponent of Indian cultural value, his services in the field of cow-breeding, research in the field of Ayurved and his practical approach of *Yoga* has won him several thousands of admirers throughout India and made him a living brand of Indian culture. Swami Ramdev was born as Ramakrishna Yadav in a very humble family of a farmer in Narnaul village at Alipur, in Mahendragarh district of Haryana, India. He studied in his Narnaul village school till 5th. He studied up to Class 8 in nearby village Shahjadpur and then joined a gurukul in Khanpur village to learn Sanskrit. Thereafter, he joined a yogic monastery (gurukul) in Khanpur village to study Sanskrit and Yoga. Eventually, he renounced worldly life and entered into Sanyas (monastic living) - taking the name Swami Ramdev. From there he went to Jind district and joined the Kalva gurukul under Acharya Baldev ji Maharaj and later imparted free Yoga training to villagers across Haryana. *Swami believed that "Yog se yeh Aaryavrat desh punah Vishva guru ke garimamay pad par pratishthit hoga" (India will again become world leader through Yoga).*

It is said that he travelled the Himalayas for several years before he settled in Haridwar. He spent a considerable amount of time in the caves of Gangotri. He discovered several medicinal plants in the Himalayas which he uses in treating his patients. After that he made persistent efforts to start Divya Yoga Mandir Trust in 1995, along with the Acharya Karamveer and Acharya Balkrishna. Baba Ramdev has a universal appeal and his customers belong to all age groups and regions. This Brand is a result of consistent hard work and carefully and meticulously followed strategy.

Baba Ramdev teaches Pranayama, a form of Yoga. The program consists of six breathing exercises, practiced in the following sequence…Bhastrika Pranayama, Kapal Bhati Pranayama, Bahaya Pranayama, Anulom Vilom Pranayama, Bhramri Pranayama and Udgeeth Pranayama.

Baba Ramdev's flagship project, the Patanjali Yogpeeth (PYP) Trust, was inaugurated on August 6, 2006. Its aim is to build the world's largest center for Ayurveda and Yoga that includes facilities for treatment, research and a teaching university. The trust primarily offers free treatment to those who cannot afford to pay. For others, treatment is provided at a lower cost than at hospitals. The service that is being provided by Baba Ramdev is well orchestrating with the desired service expectations. Patanjali Yogpeeth, a multi-million rupee venture, Ramdev's dream project, set as a rival to World Health Organization only on the basis of sound service that it boasts of providing. Not only Patanjali Yogpeeth but there is also some other departments under the brand name 'Patanjali'. They are Patanjali Yog Samiti, Patanjali Herbal Garden and Agro Research Department, Patanjali University, Patanjali Yog Science Camp. Patanjali Yog Samiti is a committee which teaches Yoga in parks and other public places like schools, temples etc. Patanjali University is for giving training of yoga, Non-residental and residential Yog science camps are conducted across the globe.

Creating a "Disease Free Society - Medicines Free World" was Swamiji's cherished dream. It is claimed that after extensive research of the valuable effects of Pranayama Yoga during last few years, on millions of people in India, it has been proved now that proper Breathing Technique's practice can cure all diseases completely without medicines or surgery. And this is the unique selling proposition of Baba Ramdev. Apart from this the customer is managed well and they eventually become brand evangelists.

Impressed by yoga guru Baba Ramdev's efforts to arouse within Biharis the urge to attain total fitness, the state government has decided to appoint him the brand ambassador of Bihar.

Yoga guru Baba Ramdev is also working towards making yoga a mass movement in the country. He claims to have trained 35,000 persons who are well equipped to hold yoga classes in different parts of the country. In the first phase of next five years, his target is to train one lakh instructors, who could impart yoga training to one crore people so that they could stay away from diseases and avoidable medication through practice of yoga. To train the yoga instructors, Pitanjali Yog Ashram has set up 535 branches and 15 more centers are in the process of being established. This is again working towards creating a new USP wherein any requirement of the customers can be catered to without delay. Baba Ramdev's potion of Pranayama is cheap. He urges people not to lose hope or suffer and depend on expensive treatments. Indian Pranayama Yoga is there to help treat all the ailments completely without costly medicines, operations or surgery.

Baba Ramdev has constantly utilized his target segment as partners in innovation, marketing and growth of his organization. He conducts effectiveness studies during his yoga camps where his staff collects on-the ground data from participants before, during and after the camp. Given the vast attendance in each of his nearly weekly camps, one can only imagine the volume of data that is collected and analyzed. He periodically revises his instructions, based on the results of ongoing research. The way his yoga camps have evolved, it is clear that he has succeeded in simplifying the efforts required to gain maximum benefits from his exercises, with enough room for flexibility and ease of involvement for the average follower.

Baba Ramdev has built some lucrative partnerships with various prominent TV channels to broadcast his yoga camps worldwide. Baba Ramdev's live yoga classes became a passion in the year 2002 when Sanskar television channel started airing Baba Ramdev's yogic classes; overnight, Baba Ramdev became a sensation he had hundreds of followers who morphed into thousands.

Then Sanskar channel's rival Astha channel signed him. In two years time he was a hit brand name and with him also the channel benefited. His TV shows have the highest TRP. Today, he is one of the biggest draws on Indian television. He can be seen not only on religious channels like Astha, but also news and features channels like India TV, Aaj tak and Sahara One.

During the camps, he routinely asks participants to get up and share their 'pranayam success stories'. Inspirational accounts from regular folks—ranging from control of diabetes, normalization of blood pressure to healthier cholesterol readings and disappearance of joint pains and skin aliments—have proved to be in valuable marketing assets for him. And best of all, they come at no cost! This is where Baba Ramdev scores heavily. He has created a great deal of self-esteem among his followers. The common attendee in his program feels special, interacts and relates to co-followers who are undergoing similar life struggles and aspirations, and gains immense confidence through perceptible and immediate self-development. Ramdev's lessons in nation building range from fighting corruption to improving our living conditions and are interjected at strategic points during his yoga instructions. In addition to humour, the swami masterfully conveys a sense of pride and possibility among his listeners.

Baba Ramdev has done no charity. Instead, he has cleverly camouflaged what could have been straightforward 'pay-per-service' such as the Art of Living programs. He charges for attending his camps but only through price discrimination. Those who can pay more are able to get better seats at the front.

Baba Ramdev has indeed created a new market. Or maybe he has simply uncovered a latent one. And yes, he has certainly accounted for the variability in cash flows of his consumers. His masterstroke has been to utilize the masses at the bottom of the income pyramid and unlocking immense value for his own projects and aspirations. By tapping into his follower's resources based on their comfort level, he is able to secure large collective donations for his gigantic yoga learning retreat in Haridwar. Not only has he effectively factored the variability in cash flows among his followers, he is also tapping into the more affluent foreign NRI segment at the moment. Baba Ramdev has used the strategy of Mass Customization to sell "Yoga" as a product to cater the needs of the masses in an era of high individual customization.

 Baba Ramdev has also introduced himself as a Business Icon. Every yoga and spiritual media channel covers Baba Ramdev for health tips and yoga, but there is more to associate with him and that is very big pharmaceutical business running in parallel named Divya Pharmacy. Although Baba never pushes people into purchasing ayurvedic medicines from his Divya Pharmacy, but it is his great marketing style that people automatically pursue to purchase. Today every pharmaceuticals company invests lot of money on advertising and marketing. Baba Ramdev is extraordinary business man who spends nothing on advertising and marketing and recruits no medical representative. He himself is the medical representative for Divya Pharmacy and he himself does the advertising. Baba Ramdev has a large number of ayurvedic products and medicine shops in their portfolio under the brand name 'Divya'. Divya Pharmacy produces different types of medicine, i.e. medicine for men, women, medicine for beauty and hair care, dental care, medicine for weight loss etc. Divya Choorn, Divya Vati, Divya

Bhasm, Divya Ras are some products of Divya Pharmacy. Baba Ramdev has turned himself into a brand element for promoting products of Divya Pharmacy. Baba's picture on product packaging generates instant trust & relevant feelings along with generating brand resonance for Divya, the pharmaceutical brand.

Also, Baba Ramdev's pack one DVD, two Video CDs written three books on Yoga, Pranayama Herbal Remedies and Magazines are available. This set of four promotional materials with a Research Oriented Monthly Magazine of Yog, Spiritualism, Ayurveda, Culture and Tradition-Yog Sandesh available in 5 languages can do much to lure customers. Even healthy people are following his Yoga Pranayama regimen, as available in his DVDs, VCDs, Books & magazines etc., to keep fit. His CDs, DVDs and audio cassettes are named as' Yog'. Some of the names of DVDs are Yog for children, Yog for weight loss, Yog for meditation, Yog for pregnant women etc.

He is also selling his products by adopting the technique of *e-marketing* as he is coming up with online shopping facilities for his customers all over the globe to make his products highly accessible.

Modern business house like Tata, Birla, Reliance are involved in social marketing as a responsibility towards the nation and humanity with Tata Memorial Hospital, Birla Temple, Reliance Education and so on. Baba Ramdev is one step ahead of these famous business houses as these business houses are primarily a business group who look into social works. Whereas Baba Ramdev is doing social services and the business is automatically growing and running.

In recent times **he has remained in lot of controversies for many claims made by him or for his medicines.** However, all these controversies have only helped in more popularizing him. **There are many critics around us who still believe that Ramdev is given much hype by the media and people then he needed.**

In January 2006, the Indian Member of Parliament Brinda Karat accused the Divya Yog Mandir Trust Pharmacy, owned by Ramdev, of using human and animal bones in their medicines. Samples of the medicines Kuliya Bhasm and Yauvanamrit Bati purchased from Brahmakalp Chikitsalay, the Trust's hospital at Haridwar, were allegedly tested at government labs which later confirmed the presence of animal materials in the sample. She exhibited the prescription and cash receipt obtained from the medicine counter in support of her claim.

Later, four samples were sent to the government-recognized Shriram Institute of Industrial Research in Delhi. The report from this institution declared that the samples did not contain objectionable ingredients and were purely herbal. Swami Ramdev was subsequently cleared of the charges.

In July 2009, in the wake of the Delhi High Court decriminalizing homosexuality in India, Ramdev told the press "The verdict will encourage criminality and sick mentality. This kind of thing is shameful and insulting. We are blindly following the West in everything. This is breaking the family system in India. Homosexuals are sick people, they should be sent to hospitals for treatment. If the government brings this law, I will take to the streets of Delhi in protest."

The makers of *Bigg Boss* are running out of idea. After boring their viewers to tears with two seasons of full-blown *nautanki* (courtesy a cheap **Rakhi Sawant** and a sleazy faux romance featuring **Monica Bedi** and **Rahul Mahajan**), they are now planning to rope none other than yoga guru extraordinaire **Baba Ramdev** who is mostly famous for his controversial statements about 'item girls and their impact on the modern youth'.

Cult figure Baba Ramdev is not only famous for his unbelievable body-bending yogic postures. But now he has an Ahmedabadbased company all tied up in knots. It's just that the company's brand name has one thing in common with the famed guru — the name Ramdev. The controversy surrounding the 'traces' of animal and human body parts found in the medicines made by Baba Ramdev's pharmacy has officials of spices maker Ramdev Food Products Pvt Ltd, which makes Ramdev Masala, hot under the collar. In fact, the loads of publicity are giving the promoters sleepless nights and they are worried about the impact on their brand equity and sales. But it was seen that Ramdev Food Products claims to have a turnover of over Rs 50 crore, including exports to UK, US, China and Australia.

India's most famous yoga guru is now working towards becoming a Media-Crazer. After taking over Aastha channel, Swami Ramdev is now all set to launch two 24-hrs channels, one will explore Indian traditional and devotional music like bhajans and the other will propagate Indian culture through the learning of the Vedas.

Although India has a long tradition of mystical gurus, Baba Ramdev represents a new phenomenon: the television yoga evangelist. As every coin has two sides, Baba Ramdev's strategies can be studied in two aspects. On one hand, his Pranayam techniques proved to be highly effective in curing a bewildering array of diseases and on the other hand he is competing with other Multi National companies in promoting yoga as a product as he calls Coke and Pepsi good only for *"Toilet- Cleaning"* on various television channels. This research reveals the power that Baba Ramdev has been able to exert over the mindsets of the people and the rapidity with which he gained approval and acceptance at all levels of the society.

By using Pranayam as a medicine he has been able to treat various incurable diseases such as Cancer, Aids, and Swine Flu etc by his extensive research in Pranayam/ Yog. So these relentless efforts of Swami Ramdev captured the masses by reviving the interest of the consumers in the age-old yogic traditions which led to the Pranayam Revolution across the globe and made this "Saffron-Clad Sanyasi" a great business tycoon.

Questions
1. Discuss the marketing mix of Swami Ramdev's products and services.
2. Discuss the Brand Identity Prism of Baba Ramdev as a Personality Brand.
3. 'Controversies aid Brand Building'- Do you agree to this statement in the context of Baba Ramdev?
4. What are the different line extensions, brand extensions and sub brands of Baba Ramdev's products and services?
5. 'Continuous Market Research serves as a fodder for a brand's sustainability'-Explain the statement in the context of the case.
6. What are the factors that have transformed Baba Ramdev into a cult brand?
7. How is Ramdev's Divya Pharmacy different from other Pharmacies?

HARRY Potter: The Multi-Billion Dollar Fictional Celebrity BRAND

It was Harry Potter and the Philosopher's Stone by J.K. Rowling published by Bloomsbury in the UK in 1997 that was found to break the jinx as far as a children's literary work witnessing significant success is concerned. The Harry Potter series was about an orphan boy with magical powers. The series was planned by Rowling to comprise of seven parts, one for each of the seven years spent by Potter at the Hogwarts School of Witchcraft and Wizardry. The novels were supposed to deal with various adventures of Potter and introduce the readers to various friends (like Ron Weasley and Hermione Granger) and enemies (like Lord Voldemort) of Potter. Harry Potter and the Philosopher's Stone tasted commercial success sans any sort of formal marketing plan. The key was that children believed that they could be Harry Potter because the character was so ordinary and easy to identify with. Word-of-mouth was the important factor triggering the sales for the book. It was personal recommendation, schoolyard conversations, Internet chat rooms, tremendous consumer satisfaction, enthusiasm and evangelism that did wonders for the book. Scholastic Inc., a US-based publisher reportedly bought the rights for the book to publish it in the US from Rowling for $1, 05,000. When the book was released in the US market, it was renamed, Harry Potter and the Sorcerer's Stone. Rowling received critical acclaims including The Young Telegraph Paperback of the Year, the British Book Awards' Children's Book of the Year, Sheffield Children's Book Award, Sorcieres Prix 1998 in France and the Premio Cento per la Letteratura Infantile 1998 in Italy.

In 1998, Bloomsbury decided to adopt the 'denial marketing policy' wherein it deliberately concealed crucial information like the publishing date for the next book from readers to add to the mystery and excitement. Harry Potter and the Chamber of Secrets was released in the UK in 1998 and in the US in 1999. The sequel proved to be a greater hit with the readers as a large number of advance orders were booked. By 1999, the two books of the Harry Potter series sold more than 5 million copies in 130 countries worldwide and they were reportedly translated into more than 25 languages. After the third sequel, Harry Potter and the Prisoner of Azkaban was released in 1999, the fourth sequel; Harry Potter and the Goblet of Fire was published in 2000. Since the release of the fourth sequel, significant marketing plans were devised by the publishers in the US and in the UK to boost the sales of the books. By late 1999, 4, 40,000 copies of the third sequel were sold in the UK. 5.3 million copies of the fourth sequel were printed and over one million copies were booked in advance. Scholastic and Bloomsbuy were found to launch a series of publicity events before the release of the fourth sequel. One among them was a four day book-signing ride across Britain. Rowling traveled on a train, Hogwarts Express (named specifically for promotion purpose) and interacted with readers at various stations across Britain. Midnight parties were arranged by the publishers as part of publicity events. Harry Potter and the Order of the Phoenix, Harry Potter and the Half-Blood Prince and Harry Potter and the Deathly Hallows were the later sequels. The sixth sequel sold 6.8 million copies in the US and 2 million copies in the UK within the first 24 hours of its release. It was quite astonishing to find that each and every sequel of the series faired better than the previous one in terms of sales and popularity among the readers. Harry Potter and the Half-Blood Prince sold 9 million copies globally within first 24 hours of its release. Commenting on the popularity of the Harry Potter series, Stephen Brown, a visiting professor of Marketing at the Northwestern University, Illinois opined in his Harvard article Marketing for Muggles:The Harry Potter way to higher profits, "The sequel eclipses the original;

the sequel's sequel eclipses the sequel; and the sequel's sequel's sequel stops the world in its orbit – a total eclipse of the market."

In 2001, the celluloid version of Harry Potter and the Sorcerer's Stone was released worldwide by Warner Bros. Daniel Radcliffe was chosen to play the role of Potter. Daniel gelled quite well with the character since he was of the same age as that of the boy mentioned in the book and his overall looks and persona seemed quite authentic.

Warner Bros. were successful in staying as close to the book as possible while depicting the various adventures of Potter on celluloid. The film went on to gross $975,800,000 worldwide. Subsequent celluloid adaptations like Harry Potter and the Chamber of Secrets (2002) and Harry Potter and the Prisoner of Azkaban (2004) grossed $869,400,000 and $789,509,413 respectively. Harry Potter and the Goblet of Fire released in 2005 earner $892 million worldwide. The four Potter films together grossed $3.5 billion worldwide. Harry Potter and the Order of the Phoenix, released in July 2007 in 4,285 US and Canadian theaters and in 44 other countries across the globe. 22000 copies of the film were shipped out our Warner Bros. studios for the international markets. The seventh and the final book of the Harry Potter series, Harry Potter and the Deathly Hallows was released worldwide on July 21st 2007. The book sold 11 million copies globally within the first 24 hours of its release.

Prior to the release of the book, the Harry Potter series had reportedly sold 325 million copies worldwide and had been translated into more than 63 languages. The books in the Potter series have been published in all sorts of formats including illustrated, Braille, audio cassette, adult cover, large print, boxed sets and so on and have been a bestseller in 120 countries across the globe. To commemorate the success of the Harry Potter series, Royal Mail, the national postal service provider in the UK commissioned a set of stamps which feature the book covers of the seven books published by Bloomsbury.

In 1998, Warner Brothers Consumer Products, after realizing the huge potential that the Harry Potter books had for merchandising and movies, bought the worldwide film, licensing and merchandising rights for Harry Potter from J.K. Rowling for $5, 00,000. In 2000, Warner Brothers signed a licensing agreement with Mattel Inc., the manufacturer of board games and toys as the master toy licensee. As per the deal, Mattel could bring out merchandising items based on the first two books of Potter as well as their celluloid versions. The agreement seemed lucrative for Warner Bros. as Mattel was present in 36 countries and sold its products in more than 150 nations. It was reported that Mattel paid a sum of

$35 million to Warner Bros and also agreed to pay 15% as royalties thereafter. Another master licensing agreement was signed with Enesco Group, a well-known US-based entity in the gifts and collectibles industry in 2000. Enesco agreed to develop gifts and collectibles based on the characters in the first three books. By late 2000, Warner Brothers reportedly granted more than 46 licenses to various other global corporate entities including Hasbro, for trading cards and candy; Electronic Arts, for video games and computer-based ancillaries; Lego, for building bricks and the Character Group for plastic and porcelain figurines. It was observed that the worldwide retail strategy for Harry Potter merchandising was carefully controlled and limited so that the Harry Potter brand did not get cheapened. While speaking to Business Wire, the global market leader in commercial news distribution on the 'controlled' worldwide marketing strategy for Harry Potter, Dan Romanelli, president Warner Brothers Worldwide Consumer Products opined, "The launch of Harry Potter products will be a worldwide effort. Our intent is to judiciously roll out the product and not to flood the market. We are looking to support the literary and film property as a long term franchise. Strategies and timing will be determined on a market by market basis."
In 2001, Warner Bros. signed Coca Cola as the sole global beverage and food marketing partner for the Harry Potter movies and the subsequent release of the videos. Coca Cola was reported to pay $287 million to Warner Brothers for the deal. Sears Roebuck & Co, a leading retail chain in the US entered into an agreement with Warner Bros. in 2001 as the principal retail partner for Harry Potter movies. Apart from launching campaigns to promote the upcoming Harry Potter movie, Sears launched Harry Potter merchandise in 860 stores across the country which included Harry Potter T-shirts, watches and bedding. By the end of 2001, the merchandising deals had earned Warner Brothers around $500 million.

The Harry Potter brand is estimated to be worth $4 billion. In terms of sales, the Harry Potter book series ranks third on the all-time bestsellers list after The Bible (2.5 billion copies) and The Thoughts of Chairman Mao (800 million). The Harry Potter franchise made a billionaire out of a struggling author named Joanne Rowling. Warner Brothers have reportedly earned $1.6 billion at the global box-office apart from $750 million it earned through DVD, video and broadcasting rights sales. More than 400 items of ancillary merchandise themed on Harry Potter are available worldwide including candy and key rings to computer games and glow-in-the-dark glasses. Many have felt that the boy wizard is Britain's biggest cultural export since the Beatles and James Bond. Pottermania has been found to have a multiplier effect on the economy as a whole. The printing industry had to stretch their work schedule to meet the first-day demands. Overnight delivery services had to put in extra effort to ensure that books reached the retailers before the official release dates. Financial experts at the Wall Street were found to hike the share prices of Scholastic and Bloomsbury to unprecedented heights especially when significant events concerning the Potter franchise took place. The Harry Potter books have been lauded to bring back the habit of reading among children of the digital age. A 24% increase in the children's book sector globally has been reported. There have also been reports of increase in applications to boarding schools in the wake of the 'Potter' phenomenon. Moreover, specific Potter vocabulary like Quidditch, Muggles, Gryffindor, Slytherin, Hogwarts have become part of the vernacular. Many have described Brand Potter as a fad but then, in this world of intense competition, almost indistinguishable products, incredible advertising clutter and increasingly marketing – savvy consumers, the brand has secured a distinct identity because of which it becomes absolutely necessary to consider the secrets of the brand's success. There have been four key factors that have contributed to the success of Harry Potter as a brand.

One of the factors that have worked in favor of Brand Potter is its narrative style of storytelling. "Tell the tale, make the sale" has been the mantra for the brand's success. An interesting observation about the Harry Potter story is that it comprises several stories. There's the story of mind blowing book selling, there's the story of the billion dollar movie franchise, there's the story of successful and relevant tie-in merchandise, there's the story of anti-witchcraft critics, there's the story of hysterical consumers, there's the story of ongoing, non-stop publicity campaign and there's also the story of 'what'll happen next' phenomenon that has been an integral part of the brand. The Harry Potter narrative proves itself to be a majestic, magical and a multi-faceted brand story. The second critical success factor for Brand Potter has been ambiguity. They have been found to appeal both to children and adults. The Harry Potter stories comprise different genres of storytelling like mystery, boarding school, coming of age etc. In some ways the stories have a modern touch and in some, they seem quite old fashioned. The stories consider the evil in good and the good in evil. They are considered "as exemplars of authentic, grassroots marketing and egregious over-exploitation by meretricious marketing types". The third success factor has been mystery. There is always that element of 'what'll happen next' both at the overarching level and within each individual volume. Each and every book of Potter has a couple of concluding explanatory chapters that are similar to the Agatha Christie whodunits. Mystery is a crucial marketing tactic which has often been found to be explored by the brand-centric organizations across the globe. The mystery, enigma and intrigue are some elements that add to the essence of a brand as it did for Harry Potter. The fourth factor that has immensely contributed to

Brand Potter's success is the entertainment value generated by the brand. The brand's personality, the reaction of the public to a book's or a film's release, the tribute websites, themed parties, long queue's outside bookstores and the marketing campaigns have all been quite entertaining. Harry Potter as a brand offers us great fun and entertainment which ensures its durability in the consumer's perceptual territory.

The Potter Marketing Philosophy eschews "the positivistic trappings of modern marketing in favor of the magical, the mysterious, the imaginative substance of postmodern marketing". Harry Potter is an icon of contemporary consumer culture and it is just a matter of time before Potter's lightning bolt (Harry Potter carries a birthmark on his forehead, which is in the shape of a lightning bolt scar) secures its place in the logo-sphere along with Nike's swoosh, Coke's copperplate curlicues and McDonald's golden arches.

Questions
1. 'Celluloid adaptation is the key to garnering more eyeballs for a literary work.' Do you agree or not? Please substantiate your answer with appropriate reference to the Harry Potter saga.
2. Explain the term 'denial marketing'. Mention its role in the propagation of Harry Potter as a leading global fictional brand.

REPOSITIONING Cadbury Dairy MILK

Cadbury Dairy Milk started its journey in the year of 1905 at Bourneville in the UK and it entered India 43 years later in the year of 1948. Over the years, the brand has established itself as the market leader in terms of market share (30%).

In the early 90's, chocolates were largely perceived as a child's heavenly dream. Children were offered chocolates as reward for good behavior or for good performance in exams. To change the mindset of Indians towards chocolates and to increase the acceptance of the brand a commercial was released by Cadbury in the mid 90's.

The commercial had the tagline "Asli Swad Zindagi Ka" ["The Real Taste of Life"]. It became very popular and redefined people's general perception towards chocolates. The objective of the commercial was to transform chocolates as a "just for kids" item to an item that appealed to the "kids in all of us". Cadbury Dairy Milk became the perfect expression of 'spontaneity' and 'shared good feelings'. The 'Real Taste of Life' campaign had many memorable advertisements, which people still fondly remember. However, the one with the "girl dancing on the cricket field" has remained etched in everyone's memory, as the most spontaneous & un-inhibited expression of happiness. With the campaign becoming a huge success Cadbury Dairy Milk was repositioned as a temptation for people of all age groups. With the passage of time, to further enhance the salience of the brand, the focus shifted towards widening chocolate consumption amongst the masses, through the "Khanewalon Ko Khane Ka Bahana Chahiye" campaign. This again repositioned Dairy Milk to be desired by anybody and at anytime.

In early 2000s, Cadbury Dairy Milk came up with a new tagline in its campaign – "Kuch Meetha Ho Jaaye" in 2000's. Through the commercials the brand wanted itself to be considered as an alternative to sweets. Dairy Milk was repositioned as a substitute for sweets through the campaign and different usage situations were highlighted through the commercials. In early 2000's the commercials stated "Dil Ko Jab Khusi Choo Jaaye, Kuch Meetha Ho Jaaye" highlighted the moments of joy to be celebrated with Cadbury Dairy Milk highlighting the habit of Indians to celebrate the joyful moments with sweets. In 2005 the "Pappu Pass Ho Gaya" commercial was released by Cadbury which became so famous that it became a part of colloquial language. The brand was endorsed by Amitabh Bachchan in the advertisement. The commercial highlighted the usage situation of celebrating an achievement or a success with a bar of Dairy Milk. The 'time of usage' tenet to reposition the flagship brand of Cadbury helped this brand to succeed in grabbing a special place in the hearts of Indians. After the "Pappu Pass Ho Gaya" campaign Cadbury continued repositioning its flagship brand Dairy Milk with different commercials based on the 'time of usage' positioning strategy. The main concept to position Dairy Milk as a substitute for sweets to celebrate any special occasion and the tagline "Kuch Meetha Ho Jaaye" were retained but different usage situations were presented.

After "Pappu Pass Ho gaya" Cadbury released popular campaigns like "Radha Miss Palampur" and "Aaj Pahli Taarikh Hai". While the first one gave the idea of having Dairy Milk after an achievement or success, the other focused on celebrating the payday with Dairy Milk.

In 2010, Cadbury Dairy Milk came up with the "Shubh Aarambh" commercials that reinforced Dairy Milk's positioning based on time of usage. Indians have the tradition of sharing sweets on auspicious occasions and also when one initiates a venture/activity. Whether the activity is small like writing an exam or huge like starting a company, sharing of sweets is an integral part of the event. The belief is that good things happen when one starts a venture on a positive note (like sharing sweets). So the campaign offers the Indians to start their special and auspicious occasions with Cadbury Dairy Milk. While the previous campaigns were narrow interpretations of "time of usage' based positioning, "Shubh Aarambh" has offered the brand a broader canvas.

Repositioning of Cadbury Dairy Milk based on 'time of usage' has helped the brand a lot in making Dairy Milk an integral part of Indians' lives. The "Shubh Aarambh" idea was further reinforced by way of non-integrated explicit product placement in KBC4 where every time a contestant was about to start the game, 'Har shubh kaam se pehle, kuch meetha ho jaaye' flashed on the TV screen. It is widely felt that the "Shubh Aarambh" campaign is the greatest idea the brand has ever come up with.

As the Indians begin their auspicious moments with sweets, this campaign has given the brand enormous opportunities to leverage this tradition. And the latest Cadbury Dairy Milk commercials are milking this idea to the fullest adding more and more value to the brand.

Questions

1. Discuss the repositioning strategy adopted by Cadbury Dairy Milk to break free from 'meant for kids' customer perception?
2. "Kuch Meetha Ho Jaaye" repositioned the brand on the product attribute. Can you suggest a better alternative to reposition the brand?
3. 'It is not advertisements but product placements along with traditional advertising that reinforce positioning statements of brands.' Do you agree? Explain stating another example of a brand apart from the one stated in the case study.

4. It is widely felt that the "Shubh Aarambh" campaign is the best among all the campaigns released by Cadbury till date. Present your own observations in this context.

CADBURY Gems Surprise: Will the new Brand Avatar CLICK?

In 2010, Cadbury launched a variant of its brand Gems named Gems Surprise. The product is a new pack of Gems that comes with a surprise toy inside. The new variant is in the shape of a ball attractively packaged. The new variant was priced at Rs 30.

Many feel that Gems Surprise is inspired by Kinder Joy. Kinder Joy is a brand marketed in India by Italian company Ferrero. The product is intended for children and is available in the form of a chocolate ball containing a small toy. Kinder Joy has been a success in various markets across the globe. The consumer acceptance of the Kinder Joy is felt to be the major reason behind the launch of Gems Surprise. Kinder Joy has largely been promoted through in-store promotions rather than promotions in the mass media.

Kinder Joy was never a competition for Cadbury Gems. Kinder Joy created a different niche where Cadbury had no brand presence. Through Gems Surprise, Cadbury intended to address the previously existing vacuum in its brand portfolio.

There is no product in Cadbury's brand portfolio that is similar to Kinder Joy. Gems was chosen because it is a unique brand with lot of equity among the consumers. The form factor of Gems also made the brand worthy of being a competitor   for   Kinder   Surprise.

Gems was always affordable and right product to buy for the Kids. Gems Surprise priced at Rs 30 is an upward stretch for the brand. However there are several uncertainties that Gems Surprise is faced with. Whether the consumer will buy Gems for Rs 30 because there is a gift free with it is a questionable area. For all those customers who has been buying SKUs of Gems for Rs 5 and Rs 10 may find it difficult to justify the purchase of Gem's Surprise at Rs 30. In the case of Kinder Joy, consumers did not have a benchmark about the price so Rs 30 for Kinder Joy was accepted by the consumer. In terms of the core product, Gems Surprise is no different from original Gems. Consumers pay more for the toy inside.

Brand analysts feel that Gems Surprise will definitely get lot of consumer trials and purchases. However the sustainability of the purchases will depend upon variety of gifts inside the Gems Surprise pack.

Questions
1. With the launch of Gems Surprise, is there a possibility of the new brand cannibalizing original Gems brand?
2. What should be the effective positioning strategy for Gems Surprise?

MARGO: The Brand's Sustainability at RISK

Margo is one of the oldest herbal soaps in India. The brand which is more than 85 years old is famous for its neem content. The brand although is synonymous with neem is increasingly being sidelined by the later entrants. For quite sometime since the launch of the brand, it had a dedicated customer base and since the product was unique due to its medicinal value, customers were found to be by and large loyal. The core brand identity of Margo was its physical attribute (composition) – neem.

With the passage of time, Margo was found to be a failure in understanding the changing dynamics of Indian consumers. More and more choices began to unfold before the Indian consumer and Margo was gradually being sidelined. Margo was positioned as "complete skin care soap". When market became fragmented with lot of products positioning based on different attributes, Margo was sidelined as a medicinal soap.

The brand had certain inherent negatives. The fragrance was not attractive nor the shape. It was also less lathering compared to its competitors. Margo changed hands from Shaw Wallace to Henkel. Although Margo was relaunched in 2003 with a new fragrance and shape, it did not quite excite the market. The brand was repositioned with the tagline: "Margo skin clear skin". The brand had a following in the states of Andhra Pradesh, Tamil Nadu and West Bengal. The brand was however found to ignore the youth segment of the Indian market.

With Lifebouy herbal variant and other established brands with neem as major content Margo's sustainability was found to be at risk. Margo needed to rejuvenate itself. The company's branding team felt that celebrity endorsement might help the brand. Rani Mukerji was roped in as the brand's face. However it was largely felt that the declining appeal of the actress among the masses proved to be a deterrent in the brand's turnaround.

Margo needs to find that 'big idea' that can not just erase the question mark on its sustainability but also gives at a fillip in terms of brand valuation.

Questions

1. 'The brand life cycle of Margo has been mismanaged'. Support the statement with adequate reasoning.
2. Many feel that Rani Mukerji was a wrong choice as brand endorser. Do you agree? If yes, then which celebrity would you feel be a better choice and why?
3. Suggest the 'big idea' that can rejuvenate Margo?

HERO Honda Pleasure: Brand Gendering in ACTION

Hero Honda launched its first scooter in November 2005 with the brand name" Pleasure". Industry insiders felt that the launch was a challenging one since the company was perceived as a bike manufacturer. It was a question of deep seated customer perception.

Pleasure is a 102 cc scooter targeting the young ladies of the country. The launch makes sense because the scooter segment is in the growth phase. It is particularly the ungeared scooter segment that is growing rapidly. With the objective of making its presence felt in this segment, Hero Honda launched Pleasure. Through Pleasure, the company is targeting Ladies and Ladies only. The scooter is being promoted with a teasing tagline- "Why should boys have all the fun?" Pleasure sells at "Just4her" showrooms which have only ladies as salespersons.

The product comes in 8 flashy colors and lots of features for the fairer sex like broader seats, electric start etc. So as far as the product concept goes, many feel that Hero Honda has a winner at hand.

The communication executed by FCB Ulka which is splashed all over the channels have an international look and aimed at the ladies in the age group of 18 – 35 years. The brand focuses on the emerging empowered ladies segment. Bollywood actress Priyanka Chopra has been roped in as the brand's ambassador. In terms of celebrity-brand fit, branding experts feel that the choice of Chopra as the brand's ambassador is perfect. Priyanka Chopra exudes confidence and a liberated attitude in the advertisements.

There are some issues of concern for Pleasure. The product is pitted against Honda Activa and Dio. Activa is a formidable player and its reputation itself is an entry barrier for Pleasure. Since the pricing of Pleasure is comparable with that of Dio, Pleasure need to make sure that it creates a meaningful differentiation.

As per industry reports, many of Hero Honda's brand launches since the mid 2000s have been failures. It remains to be seen if Hero Honda can launch a winner in Pleasure by adopting gender based branding strategy.

Questions

1. Hero Honda has taken gender based branding route for its Pleasure. Give an account of another brand that has taken a similar route (same or from a different industry)?

2. As a student of marketing, do you feel that Pleasure will be a success for Hero Honda? Explain with suitable reasoning.

MCDONALD'S and Global BRANDING

McDonald's is the leading global food retailer with 30,000 restaurants serving 50 million people in 119 countries every day. Half of all McDonald's restaurants are located outside the US, and more than 50% of the company's operating income is derived from them. McDonald's had forayed into international markets by expanding its business into Canada and Puerto Rico in 1967 due to its domestic market saturation. In the emerging markets, McDonald's adopted the franchising route as its entry strategy. It is observed that two reasons have enabled McDonald's to successfully localize across different continents. First, McDonald's has always depended on local businesses like local contractors, food suppliers and financial institutions. Second, the company has consistently voiced its concern for the well-being of its guests in various ways over the years apart from actively supporting local charity work and community programs.

Across the globe, 70% of McDonald's restaurants are owned and operated by independent, local businessmen. For expanding into different markets, McDonald's obtains much of its required funding from multinational and local banks. It is cited that the formula for McDonald's global growth has been developing markets as long-term investments and cultivating reliable local suppliers, who ensure that food items and raw materials are transported fresh and safe. McDonald's also actively involves local business people, and make them a part of the success story in whichever country they do business. For example, in France, McDonald's teamed up with several local companies to offer local items like fruit yogurts produced by Danone, coffee from Carte Noire and the French soft drink Orangina. McDonald's buys 80% of its products from French farmers and advertises in local dailies highlighting the number of French cows, chicken, lettuce and tomatoes it uses every year. McDonald's strategy has always been to be close to people in its country of operation and modify itself to communicate meaningfully to the local populace. While many brands globalize logos, brand names and trademarks, and introduce product variations at the local level, McDonald's has been accepted as a local brand in most markets where it operates.

In Israel, McDonald's replaced its highly recognizable "Golden Arches" and the red and yellow signs mentioning "McDonald's" with blue and white Hebrew lettering in some of its restaurants. It also mentioned the word "*kosher*" (meaning meat for which an animal has been slaughtered as per Jewish law) alongside, after Tel Aviv's chief rabbi refused to certify the restaurants as kosher unless McDonald's designated them so. The chief rabbi stated that he did not want that those who followed a kosher diet to accidentally dine at a non-kosher outlet as not all restaurants follow the Jewish law of keeping meat and dairy products separate.

McDonald's entered China in 1990, a decade after the commencement of the economic reforms in the country and people were positive about foreign investments. By the mid-1990s, there were several McDonald's restaurants at Beijing as the people loved the convenience, efficient service, comfortable environment, soothing music and a casual atmosphere at these restaurants.

In India, though McDonald's expansion happened faster compared to other Southeast Asian countries like Indonesia, the company had to face certain hurdles initially. The company faced customers with highly diverse food culture; with 20% of the population being pure vegetarian and 82% non-beef eaters. Besides, people do not prefer frozen meat and are generally fond of spicy dishes of fish. People viewed McDonald's as a *videsi* (The word videsi in Hindi means something or someone related to a foreign country) version of local fast food retailers charging prohibitive prices. McDonald's also failed to understand the food preferences of its Indian customers. The company also faced oppositions from various quarters regarding environmental and animal welfare issues. Vandana Shiva, a former director of the Research Foundation for Science, Technology and Natural Resource Policy (a network of researchers specializing in sustainable agriculture and development) strongly objected McDonald's entry into

India citing, apart from other issues, that it was promoting child labor across the world. She observed that McDonald's ushers in a culture of eating junk food, which in the long run, could adversely affect people's diet and health.

To overcome these hurdles, McDonald's localized its menu and introduced non-beef and non-pork products in the Indian market. It made efforts to mix and adapt two food cultures, American and Indian, which led to the development of the successful Maharaja Mac. Since 1997, McDonald's has grown at a rate of 50% annually and has established itself in the west and north of India. McDonald's has also adopted an aggressive pricing policy, branding it as the "Happy Price Menu" where a number of products are provided to customers at a nominal INR 20 (INR stands for Indian Rupee). This has helped McDonald's to reach out to a wider cross-section of the Indian population.

To be a Quick Service Restaurant leader, McDonald's India (North) has started an innovative delivery system for the residents of Chandni Chowk in Delhi. It's called "McDelivery on Bicycles" which has been started keeping in view the maze of bylanes in the area. As an introductory offer, customers are entitled to complimentary Chicken McGrill or a McAloo Tikki burger on any order from the McDelivery at Chandni Chowk.

It is observed that McDonald's proactiveness in its localization strategies has differentiated it from its competitors. Based on demography, it has also come out with innovative localization strategies on its own to constantly maintain the freshness of its brand by attracting newer segments in the existing markets, bringing in more traffic to its restaurants, providing the McDonald's experience to people at the most unexpected places or communicating to the target audience according to local tastes and temperaments.

For example, in China, where McDonald's opened its first restaurant in 1990, 100 restaurants use the Chinese characters *"Mai Dang Lao"* to phonetically mean the word "McDonald's". Besides, McDonald's is seen as a place for social activities and celebration of various occasions by families (the incidence of children's birthdays are very high). McDonald's restaurants in China ensure a Chinese-family atmosphere, gives priority to family values and hires inter-generational workers. The fast food retailer also relies on manual operations unlike what it does in the US where it is known for its mechanized operations.

In Japan, the largest market for McDonald's outside the US, McDonald's has aggressively followed the strategy of reducing the prices of its offerings to gain more market share. Fujita (the Chairman of McDonald's Japan), who was instrumental in bringing McDonald's to Japan in 1971 through a joint venture with the US parent company, carefully shaped the brand image with commercials that had the essence of American commercials with local flavor. American flags and other articles promoting Americanism were kept out of the restaurants. The name McDonald's was also spelled in Japanese, which was *"Mack-u-dona-rudo"*. In 1995, McDonald's Japan began to aggressively reduce prices after it ran a hamburger promotion, and witnessed sales leap by 20%.

McDonald's core principles are quality, service, cleanliness and value (better known as the QSCV principle). It has been committed to provide its customers quality products promptly with a smile, in a pleasant and clean surrounding and all at a fair price. McDonald's "Plan to Win" strategy has been a global alignment around five drivers of outstanding customer service (which can also be called the 5Ps. They are products, people, place, price and promotion). These have ensured a common brand identity for McDonald's globally.

Despite its efforts to promote a unified global brand, there have been instances when McDonald's introduced new elements in its menu to appeal to local tastes. In 1971, when the first European outlet was opened in the Netherlands, the menu included breaded meatball krokets. While in Australia a McOz Burger was introduced with a slice of beetroot, in Japan, Pork teriyaki33 was introduced. Some other examples are "McHuevo" in Uruguay (which is a hamburger with a poached egg on top), "McLaks" in Norway (which is a grilled salmon sandwich with dill sauce), "Samurai Pork Burger" in Thailand (which is a sausage patty in teriyaki sauce).

In India, due to abstinence from beef-eating, McDonald's serves "Maharaja Mac", an all ground lamb burger with lettuce, tomatoes, special sauce, cheese, onion and pickles on a sesame bun. The vegetarian items are advertised with a "100% pure veg" stamp on them. As Indians like spices, McDonald's introduced sauces like McMasala and McImli to satisfy Indian taste buds and have reformulated some products like McVeggie burger, McAloo Tikki burger, Veg Pizza McPuff and Chicken McGrill burger by using spices. It has also created egg less sandwich sauces for vegetarian customers. Even the soft serves and McShakes are egg less offering larger variety to vegetarian customers who constitute a considerable chunk in this country.

Commenting on McDonald's global branding strategy, one of the company's insiders opined, "The business at McDonald's is much more about local relevance than a global archetype. Globally we think of ourselves as the custodian of the brand but it's all about relevance to the local markets."

Questions

1. What are the various reasons cited in the case study that have made McDonald's global branding a success?
2. Comment on McDonald's branding strategy in the Indian sub-continent?

SECTION – II

CASE Studies on Services MARKETING

EAT on the GO

Eat on the Go was a popular among the foodies of Delhi in the 1990s. The concept behind the mobile eating joint was simple and unique. *Eat on the Go* used to serve people on mobile vans at various locations of the city that had a cluster of companies. The company behind the fast food brand was Harmesh Associates. *Eat on the Go* served vegetarian meals and was mainly aimed at serving breakfast, lunch and evening snacks to those working in various companies. It was felt that people often were unable to have proper food in the morning while moving out for their offices. Also many of them were unable to carry food along with them. The service was mainly aimed at those people. It was observed that people by and large were happy with the range of food available and the quality of the food.

However since early 2000s, when the fuel prices started rising steeply, Harmesh Associates felt that mobile vans that ran on fuel were not quite a cost effective proposition since the rates of food were on the cheaper side and the operational costs were higher than the revenues earned in most cases. The company that used to run 15 mobile vans reduced the number of to just five and those were found to serve only the high traffic zones.

Harmesh Associates further took the initiative to opening retail joints at various happening junctions of the city and those were named *Eat on the Go* too. The joints had a similar menu and their timings were similar to that of the mobile vans. After six months of this initiative, it was observed that the joints were unable to register significant footfalls. Moreover, the traffic being served by the mobile vans also went down drastically.

Harmesh Associates were at a loss to understand what went wrong. They did not feel that reach was the issue neither did they feel that the quality of food or the quality of manpower was the issue. Then what was the actual issue(s)?

Questions:
1. What was/were the issues involved that led to reduction in customer footfalls for Harmesh Associates?

2. Do you feel that if *Eat on the Go* would have been restricted to mobile vans only along with altering the menu or rates, it would have been a better ploy?
3. What are your suggestions for Harmesh Associates to regain lost ground?

PIZZA ETCETERA

Pizza Etcetera is a restaurant in the Sector V area of Kolkata that serves pizzas along with coffee and soft drinks. The Sector V area is known to house several IT giants of the country like TCS, CTS, Wipro, IBM and many more. The restaurant had a great rage of pizzas along with having beautiful décor and great courteous staff members. The ambience of the restaurant was further enhanced by the background music being played at the store at different times of the day. The restaurant was generally found to attract lots of footfalls during the day time especially during the 12 noon to 3 PM slot.

However it was observed that people had to wait in long queues to get their order registered with the cashier and they had to wait further to get their orders served. Moreover the number of seats available within the restaurant was extremely less compared to the number of customers that visited the restaurant during the 12 noon to 3PM slot. The management at Pizza Etcetera felt that pizza as such was not such an item where customers needed to seat as such. They could very well enjoy their food while standing and chatting. After all, it was the employees working at various offices who frequented at that juncture and they would like it that way. However there were many customers who expressed their displeasure with the system. They also complained regarding the lot waiting hours to be served.

Another cause of concern for the Pizza Etcetera management was that barring the 12 noon to 3PM slot, the restaurant was largely vacant. There were very few customers who came to the outlet and thus operational costs were on the higher side compared to the total daily revenues generated.

The management had two major issues to address else it was destined to fail in the long run.

Questions:
1. Comment on the marketing mix of Pizza Etcetera?
2. Mention the two major issues to be handled by the management at Pizza Etcetera?
3. As a consultant, what suggestions for improvement would you prescribe to the management at Pizza Etcetera to enhance their operational efficiencies?

BHUSHAN TELECOM

Bhushan Telecom Services was to first company to offer mobile services to the people of Bokaro, one of the reputed industrial towns in the state of Jharkhand. The company was the sole mobile service provider for the people of the city between 1999 and 2002. The customers were happy with the connectivity, clarity and coverage being offered by Macho, the brand name for mobile services offered by Bhushan Telecom.

However in early 2004, national mobile service providers like Hutch and Reliance entered the city with their host of talk plans and infrastructure. Soon the magic behind the brand names started having negative impact on Bhushan Telecom. People were more interested to try out the national mobile service providers since they offered a better coverage and offered lots of exciting incentive schemes. Bhushan Telecom neither had the infrastructure to provide nation wide coverage nor had they got the deep pockets of offering range of incentive schemes to customers from time to time.

Bhushan Telecom needed to survive and survive well. After all they could not let go the initial edge they had over competition. The management decided to take the new entrants head on by lowering the call rates drastically. Company insiders felt that the move was definitely not sustainable. It was observed that the customers for Bhushan Telecom were least interested with the move and viewed Macho as copying the strategies of the new entrants. It was further observed that the connectivity and clarity took a back seat with the lowering of call rates. It was soon found that large chunk of customers at Bokaro perceived Bhushan Telecom as a 'dead' company. Can a rejuvenation of brand Macho be possible?

Questions:
1. What were the problem areas of Bhushan Telecom?
2. Assume yourself to be the newly appointed VP-Marketing at Bhushan Telecom. What will be your suggestions to improve the state of the company and its market share?
3. Instead of taking head on, what could have been a better marketing strategy for Bhushan Telecom to tackle new competitors?

HEAD TURNERS

Head Turners is a beauty salon who specializes in styling hair of both men and women. They have started their operations couple of months back in the city of Hyderabad and exist at four of the most happening destinations of the city viz. Panjagutta, Banjara Hills, Jubilee Hills and Dilsukhnagar. Head Turners went for aggressive promotions prior to the launch of their outlets in various parts of the city. The company positioned the brand as The Best Hair Styling Experts in Town. Naturally the target audience had an expectation that Head Turners will be the place where the services of the most effective hair stylists will be on offer.

Head Turners had outlets that were simply dazzling. They had great interiors, great lighting, great gizmos along with great background music. In short, the ambience was perfect at each and every outlet. The problem however was at a more crucial level. The employees who were servicing the customers were expected not just to be courteous but also immensely skilled. After all that was the very positioning strategy of the company.

First hand experiences of various customers were just the reverse. They were quite happy with the ambience and other associated factors including the pricing. But then they complained about the staff members who were not suitably skilled to handle various jobs. Moreover, when any customer pointed out their mistakes, they became furious at times and mentioned that they knew their job and they do not need to learn from customers. There were several service gaps identified at Head Turners. It was found that the 'People' factor at Head Turners was the major reason why customers did not feel to visit the outlets the second time after their first visit.

Questions:
1. What were the problem areas regarding the service marketing mix at Head Turners?
2. What were the service gaps existing at Head Turners?
3. What are the strategies that you would suggest Head Turners to improve their image and enhance customer loyalty?

NORTH Star Hotel PLAZA

North Star Hotel Plaza is a luxury hotel located on the EM Bypass area in Kolkata. The hotel started its operations in the year 1990 and since then it has been a favorite destination for the elite class. While local customers have frequented the two major restaurants of the hotel viz. Tulip and Macarani, the tourists who have come to Kolkata have preferred North Star over other hotels in the city. The hotel has been known for great food and décor along with extremely courteous staff members. The hotel is known to serve authentic Bengali food along with serving vegetarian meals of various eastern and north eastern states of the country. It was reported that customer footfalls increased from 10% to 30% during the 1992-1996 period.

However post 2005, North Star has been facing tremendous competition from other premium hotels like the ITC Sonarbangla and Hyatt Regency that have come up in the area and are attracting various customers with deep pockets along with hosting various important events and seminars. There was not much variation in the room types offered by North Star nor did the hotel authorities feel the need to promote the hotel and keep the aura of the hotel alive in the media. With more options being offered by the later entrants, customers both local and tourists were found to stay away from the hotel. This led to drastic reduction in customer footfalls and that had a negative impact on the revenues earned by the hotel.

A top level meeting was organized to do a post mortem of the matter. The overall opinion was that North Star Hotel Plaza did not do much to reposition its offer over the years. It's arrogance and ignorance were the main causes of its downfall and something needed to be done fast before it was too late.

Questions:
1. What were the causes for the increase in footfalls at North Star during the 1992-1996 period?
2. What were the problem areas faced by North Star?
3. What were the shortcomings in the marketing mix of North Star that led to the decline in customer footfalls?
4. Mention some strategies that can enable North Star to regain lost ground?

THE Café SHOP

The Café Shop opened its first outlet at the national level in Bangalore in the year 2000. Within a span of 5 years, the coffee retailer expanded its business in the states of Andhra Pradesh, Gujarat, Maharashtra, West Bengal and Tamil Nadu. Right from day one, the coffee retailer was found to focus on the quality of its core product – coffee apart from focusing on the ambience of its outlets. It believed that consistency in customer experience was the key to sustainability and hence the management ensured that customers had similar experience in terms of ambience, staff behavior and quality and range of products wherever they went. Thus each outlet offered the same variants of coffee, had the same courteous and knowledgeable staff and had the similar décor and ambience in terms of background music and the sight and smell of the store.

Since 2006 however, The Café Shop witnessed lots of competition in the coffee retailing domain. The teenage and youth segment were found to like the idea of having coffee along with friends and family both during weekends as well as during weekdays. Unlike the restaurants, coffee retailing entities had almost uniform footfalls throughout the week. With the coming up of coffee retailing entities like Fresh and Honest, Silverline, Mocha, Caffeine and others, The Café Shop witnessed a dip in its footfalls for the first time in 2007 followed by 2008.

The management took up the matter seriously and decided upon conducting a market survey to understand the pulse of the evolving consumer base. What emerged from the study was that The Café Shop needed to reposition its offer along with offering certain add ons apart from serving quality coffee along with great ambience. From positioning its outlets as *Your Friendly Café Shop*, it repositioned its positioning statement to *Coffee and More..*clearly indicating that the outlets had something more to offer to customers. Not only that, various reality shows on MTV were being sponsored by The Café Shop that clearly highlighted its youth connection. Several contests were held for the customers from time to time that enhanced their engagement with the retail brand. A tabloid meant only for in-shop consumption was launched which was placed at each and every table of The Café Shop outlets which contained news items on movies, politics, sports, literature etc. This ensured that customers stayed for longer periods of time at the coffee shops. This in turn often meant higher ticket size per customer visit.

The Café Shop was also found to include certain additional products like chocolates, cookies, cakes and pastries that could be either consumed in-shop or could be taken by the customers for their home consumption. The strategy worked for The Café Shop as it was found to have a healthy edge over competition having a market share of around 80% in the year 2011.

Questions:
1. Comment on the revamped marketing mix at The Café Shop?
2. Identify the various factors that have triggered the growth of coffee shops in the country over the years?

3. Assume yourself to be the owner a retail brand that is placed 2nd in terms of market share. What strategies will you devise for your company to offset the advantage being enjoyed by The Café Shop?

ONLINEMATRIMONY.COM

Onlinematrimony.com is a site owned by M/s Simcon Associates. The company launched the website in the 1998 and over the years, it has been found to continuously add on new members to the site. The company behind the website understood the importance of having offline offices along with the online services being offered to enhance trust among the customer base. The company thus initially opened offices at all the major metros of the country followed by couple smaller towns of the country like Baroda, Gwalior and Ranchi.

Within couple of years of onlinematrimony.com's launch, there were similar websites that came to the limelight and these too were found to go for lots of aggressive advertising and generating significant customer responses. Some of the websites even had great emotional messages to deliver through their advertisements and slogans. However, Simcon Associates believed that proper segmentation was the key to business sustainability and hence they within years of launch, went about creating newer sub domains of their parent web address. The new websites that were offshoots of the parent catered to specific needs of various communities among the Hindus of the country like the Brahmin community and the kshatriya community. There were also web addresses that catered to the customized requirements of the Mangliks, the Rarhi class of the Brahmins etc. It was found that onlinematrimony.com actually had a much greater and bigger reach compared to competition due to its segmentation strategy.

With the increase in the usage of the Internet in the country and people's comfort using the net, newer avenues of interactions among the registered members of the website were devised like chats, sms and mms. Simcon Associates maintained its belief that both online as well as offline interactions with and among the registered members of the site was important and hence while online matrimony meets were arranged every month, there were offline meets arranged for various communities every six months.

While Onlinematrimony.com had registered members to the tune of 20,5012 in December 2011, its nearest competitor Indiamatrimony.com had 13,7721 registered members. Onlinematrimony.com enjoyed leadership position in the online matrimonial services market both in terms of share of mind and share of voice.

Questions:
1. What were the major reasons for Onlinematrimony.com's success?
2. Do you really feel that a service entity like onlinematrimony.com needs to have offline interactions with its customer base along with online interactions? Give reasons for your opinion?
3. As the CEO of Indiamatrimony.com, would you take onlinematrimony.com head on to combat competition? State reasons for your response along with specifying strategies to be adopted by you to revamp your market share?

SECTION – III

CASE Studies on Retail MARKETING

A Tale of Two STORES

*T*he *Daily Mart*, a food and grocery retail shop was opened at Panjagutta (Hyderabad) in 2001. The area had a mixture of business establishments as well as residential apartments. Shopping at supermarkets for daily needs was new in India at that point. The owner of the shop Bhusan Reddy believed in the first-mover advantage and so he made it a point that his retail format was the first in the area. As time went by, his belief paid rich dividends as footfalls multiplied and there were many who frequented the shop almost on a regular basis. The story remained much the same for the next two years.

In early 2004, *Onions Etcetera* a food and grocery retail shop was established in the same area by the Sri Sai Business Group. *Onions Etcetera* was just bang opposite to where *The Daily Mart* was existing for more than two years. Within six months of *Onions Etcetera* starting its operations, Reddy found the sales revenues of his business declining steadily. The trend continued for few more months and Reddy started pondering as to what was the reason behind the same. The customers who earlier used to frequent *The Daily Mart* now preferred shopping at *Onions Etcetera* on a daily basis. Reddy first tried to compare the price of offerings in the two shops and found that it was his shop that had an edge. The overall exterior and interior décor was also much the same. In terms of product range, it was *The Daily Mart* that was the clear winner. Reddy's enterprise adopted scrambled merchandising strategy as it was felt that this could attract additional shoppers. Magazines, CDs, wallets and few fashion accessories and toys were added. But hardly any positive development was identified.

Bhushan Reddy hired a retail consultant to seek a panacea to the problem. The consultant, Anand Mali after studying the operations of the two competing shops identified that the problem lay with the sales and service staff of *The Daily Mart* and also the merchandise placement strategies adopted by Reddy. While the CSAs of *Onions Etcetera* were a highly motivated, well skilled, courteous and well groomed individuals, the personnel at Reddy's enterprise were shabbily dressed, moron creatures on whose faces it was always written-"its just another day. What's new about it?" The traits of ambition, commitment, persuasiveness and passion were simply not to be found among them. This caused customers to switch once they had a better option. Moreover, the aisles were too narrow which often made one feel as if he/she was in a well illuminated warehouse and not quite in a retail store. The placement of merchandise was such that it allowed very little scope for the CSAs to go for upselling or cross selling. For example, the place where potatoes were kept and the potato peelers existed were far off which eliminated the scope of selling a peeler as a complimentary item along with potatoes. Customers were simply not interested to go that 'extra mile' to shop for a potato peeler. Merchandise were generally dumped on racks. Many FMCG items could have well been presented as blocks. Color blocking would have greatly enhanced the visual appeal.

Mali's feedback proved to be an eye opener. But then Reddy was not at ease. He knew he had lots to do before he could really pose to be a threat to his competitor.

Discussion Questions:

'An ineffective employee is actually a liability to his/her employer'. Do you agree to this statement? Explain with reference to the case study.

Effective merchandise presentation in case of supermarkets can be a better alternative to enhancing store revenues rather than overall visual merchandising of a store. Debate.

Apart from the suggestions offered by Anand Mali, will you like to suggest few other alternatives to Bhushan Reddy that can enhance his store's revenues?

VIGNESH Movies: Pricing Strategies of the Entertainment RETAILER

Vignesh Movies Private Limited was among the first cinema exhibitors in the country that went about establishing multiplex chains in the country. Way back in the year 1997, Vignesh Movies was found to establish the first multiplex at Andheri in Mumbai. It went for continuous expansion since then not just in the city of Mumbai but also in smaller towns of Maharashtra like Pune, Nasik and

Kolhapur. The company's CEO, Mr. Anand Parikh was spot on in understanding the fact that the potential customers of his multiplex would not just come to the theatres to watch movies but to seek experiences and so he concentrated on recruiting the right kind of work force who would function as ushers during the shows along with creating the right sort of ambience for customers.

However, since the mid 2000s, Mr. Parikh observed that there were a number of companies that were entering the business of cinema exhibition and he understood that apart from offering the right service quality, he would need to focus on a competitive pricing strategy that would enhance footfalls to the multiplex chain.

Pricing a movie ticket was a difficult proposition and Vignesh Movies believed in providing high quality movie viewing at an affordable price. But then rising input costs like wages, rent, electricity and others made Mr. Parikh pensive about what should be the ideal business and pricing model. A major restructuring exercise was initiated where the services of Vignesh Movies were divided into Vignesh Premier, Vignesh Class and Vignesh Economy. It was further decided the comfort and hospitality provided in the two formats would vary. The prices of tickets in the three formats during weekends were Rs 500, Rs 350 and Rs 200 respectively for Hindi and English movies. The price per ticket for regional movies ranged from Rs 80 to Rs 150. The prices of Vignesh Class and Vignesh Economy were different on weekdays than what they were on weekends. However, the pricing of tickets for Vignesh Premier was the same. Watching any movie at Vignesh Economy before 12 noon would cost Rs 50 per ticket. Out of Rs. 500 that was charged for Vignesh Premier, Rs. 350 was the price of movie viewing and the rest was for the snacks that were provided to customers. It was believed that customers had the best experience when they got to much something along with movie viewing.

The exercise clicked and it was later found by Mr. Parikh and his team that bundling of snacks along with movie viewing and differential pricing based on hospitality provided and the day of the week were some that allowed Vignesh Movies to enjoy a competitive edge over the later entrants.

Discussion Questions:

What is the pricing strategy adopted by Vignesh Movies?

Does bundling the movie ticket and food and beverages help in creating a positive brand image in the minds of customers? Justify with appropriate examples.

Can you suggest Mr. Parikh certain improvisations in the context of pricing policy or business policy that can enhance his business revenues?

GOING the Private Label WAY

Express Holdings Private Limited entered the business of food and grocery retailing in the year 2007 under the brand name Swastik. Swastik had religious connotations as a name. At the same time, the word was considered auspicious and it was attached to domestic well being. As a brand name thus, the parent company had full faith in the brand naming process.

By the time Swastik created awareness among the target customers about itself at a pan-Indian level, there were a host of supermarket brands already present in the Indian retailsphere. Brands like Food Bazaar, Spencer's, Subhiksha were going great guns. Moreover, the Indian customers were still used to shopping at bazaars and kirana stores which further added to the woes of the management.

Swastik retailed all the reputed national brands as far as grocery items were concerned. It had an extremely well trained staff who were adept in product knowledge and retail selling skills. The ambience of the Swastik stores was quite inviting and the prices were competitive. But then a market survey proved that Swastik was considered a 'me-too' brand in the food and grocery retailing arena. There was a strong need to differentiate to stay in the race.

After several brainstorming sessions, it was decided that Swastik would by and large manufacture and retail its own brands as far as grocery items were concerned. This would help Swastik save on the costs of manufacturing and transporting the goods and the benefits of the savings could be passed on to the customers. Moreover they would be adopting an effective communication strategy that would make customers understand the fact that they would get quality products at lesser prices compared to national brands. Indians by and large are quite price sensitive when it comes to shopping for food and grocery items.

The private label strategy was initially implemented in some Swastik outlets on a pilot basis and it was found that the company saved on costs of manufacturing and transportation of goods. Also the lead time involved between the placement of an order and receiving it at the stores was greatly reduced. The perishables were received fresh and sold fresh at the stores and customers did found value in shopping at Swastik stores. Within a few months the private label strategy was implemented across all the Swastik stores of the country and the move was found to bring in significant revenues for the company.

Discussion Questions:
How important do you think is private label strategy in the context of food and grocery retailing?

Do you think that the behavior of Indian consumers is actually a hurdle for the development of supermarket chains in the country? Explain with adequate reasoning.

Enumerate some of the common customer perceptions or misperceptions regarding private labels?

What are the various advantages of private label strategies for retailers?

Can u suggest few other aspects that can enhance the revenues for Swastik?

ONLY Snacks & Retail FRANCHISING

Chamanbhai Mehta is a 35 year old high school drop out but has a business acumen that any top B-school graduate would envy. Since 2005, he has successfully expanded his fast food chain named Only Snacks across the length and breadth of the country. He started his business from his hometown in Ahmedabad and soon expanded via the franchising route in the states of Maharashtra, Karnataka, Madhya Pradesh and Rajasthan. There was a simple and noble idea behind his fast food business. Nuclear families where both husband and wife are working are increasing exponentially in India and this development has disallowed many to prepare their breakfasts at home. There are many who prefer to take their breakfasts on the drive and this is what Mehta's business offered.

Quality Indian snacks, prepared hygienically, offered to customers who had to wait the least amount of time for being served. Chamanbhai can well be compared to the legendary Ray Kroc of McDonald's for having the vision and the will power to turn a pretty simple idea into a big time business. Mehta was clear about one thing that there were Indians who would prefer to have breakfasts on the go but then it was not possible for him financially to expand on his own. He needed people who would accept and acknowledge his business model and would invest in it. This propelled Mehta to invite franchisees for his business. He would travel to various places where potential franchisees would be invited for a seminar. They would be briefed about the business, its present state of finances, its potential. Mehta would make sure that franchisees were informed about each and everything before they signed the dotted line.

India is a land of diverse religion and cultures and so each state had its own unique ways of food consumption. While Mehta ensured that his franchisees stuck to the core idea of offering quality, hygienic food at the least possible time to customers, they were given the liberty in hiring the manpower, communicating to target customers in the mass media in a way they felt the best and experiment with the menu. In the long run, the franchising strategies of Chamanbhai were found to create a 'win-win' scenario for both the franchisor and the franchisees.

Discussion Questions:

From the case study, identify the franchisor and the franchise?
Comment on Chamanbhai's approach to franchising?
Will you like to recommend any strategy to Chamanbhai that could enhance his business revenues?
Do you really think that Chamanbhai's business can have a pan-Indian appeal? Explain with proper reasoning.

VISUAL Merchandising Gone WRONG!

Ankit Jain, son of a very successful Delhi-based businessman decided to venture into the business of speciality retailing after his MBA. Café shops had always earned a special place in his heart since his college days and so he decided to open a café shop near Vikaspuri.

Location wise, Café Point, Ankit's brainchild was perfect. The place was in the vicinity of several management and general colleges. Also, there were various shopping malls and big brand retail stores near by. In short, the café shop was ensured of garnering both eye balls as well as footfalls. The exterior presentation of the store was perfectly done. The exterior sign along with well defined walks and entry with some amount of landscaping in front was just perfect for any potential customer to drop in and check out the shop and its services.

Ankit had a friend who was in a placement consultancy firm who helped him source the right kind of manpower for Café Point. The service staffs were found to be quite skilled in customer service and product knowledge. Café Point, apart from offering Coffee also offered pizzas, burgers, pastries, fruit juices etc. It was found that during the day, Café Point mainly had visitors who were college goers but in the evenings or during the weekends, there were many families who were frequenting the shop.

The color scheme that Ankit decided upon for his shop was grey interiors and the dresses of his service staff were also of the same color to bring in consistency.

The mats on the tables were also of the grey color and the shop was dimly illuminated most of the time. Instrumental music was mostly played at the shop.

After a span of some 3-4 months, Ankit noticed that there was hardly any additional footfall in the store. Actually footfalls had dropped and most of the customers who visited the shop were new faces. It meant that people who had once experienced the shop did not feel like coming back which was quite contrary to what is observed among customers in the context of café shops. They generally like to hang out at their favorite café shops. What was wrong? Ankit pondered. He had a great service staff, had a competitive menu and above all, his shop was at a great location.

Discussion Questions:

Comment on the retail marketing mix adopted by Ankit Jain for Café Point?

Identify the shortcomings in the visual merchandising strategy adopted by Ankit?

What are your recommendations that will allow Ankit to enhance footfalls at his shop and make repeat customers visit Café Point?

INEFFECTIVE Mall MANAGEMENT

It was 2001 and the concept of malls in India was pretty new at that point of time. Ramnik lal Joshi, a noted industrialist and CEO of RLJ Group went ahead with his decision to open a mall in Faridabad, a place close to the Indian capital and also well connected to some of posh localities of Noida and Gurgaon. The mall was named *The RLJ Orbit Mall*. It was four storied mall with around three to four well known exclusive stores like Weekender, Adidas, Provogue and Peter England. A super market was also to be found within the mall called K-Mart. The mall had a concoction of several retail formats dealing in several product categories. There was almost everything more everyone. The mall had a two-screen multiplex (Vasant Theatres) in the 2nd and 3rd floors while the food court was on the ground floor.

The apparel retailers along with other retail formats were mainly on the top floor. The mall had an elevator but no escalator as such. Due to the presence of just one elevator, it often resulted in huge commotion especially during start and end of movie shows. Parking was another problem for the visitors plus safety with their vehicles was also an issue.

Many retailers found that there were hardly any footfalls on a daily basis. Very few visitors even bothered to take a look at what was there on the top floor. They either left from the ground floor itself or at most came to the third floor for viewing a movie. The mall was located in a posh area and so its rental was quite high which had to be borne by the retailers present in the mall which further added to their woes.

The retailers were not happy. They were contemplating to leave the mall and set shop elsewhere but then a huge investment was already lost. Ramnik Lal Joshi himself was also not a happy man. He wanted to do something new; something that would fetch him great revenues but here he was facing a situation that was not just discouraging but threatening too. Ramnik Lal Joshi needed to rethink certain things and redo a lot.

Discussion Questions:

What were the problem areas of *The RLJ Orbit Mall*?

Is a great location enough for a mall's well being or are there various other factors that need to be looked at? What are those factors?

In India, retailers at malls are often faced with the situation of escalating rentals and descending footfalls? Suggest ways to tackle this critical issue?

SECTION – IV

CASE Studies on Sales MANAGEMENT

Eureka!

In 1999, Eureka Forbes Ltd. (Eureka Forbes), the leading vacuum cleaner and water/air purifier equipment company, announced a major policy change that came as a surprise to the Indian corporate world. The company, regarded as the pioneer of direct marketing in India, was planning to focus more on the retailing business in the future. Commenting on this decision, S Goklaney, Managing Director, Eureka Forbes, said, "Direct sales permits us to exploit only the top end of the market." This move was in accordance with the company's plans to increase the visibility of its products. The company planned to make its products available in retail outlets through its dealer network, spread across 2,600 dealers.

With this move, Eureka Forbes also planned to increase the sales revenue generated by the retail division. Eureka Forbes Senior Vice-President, Sales and Marketing, Palekar, explained, "While the dealer channel contributes 10% to the overall sales turnover of the company, the direct sales route contributes 75%."

The same year, in another major departure from the business practices adopted since it began business in India, Eureka Forbes announced its decision to enter the bottled water market. The company wanted to position itself as a one-stop shop for products related to providing pure water.

Industry watchers questioned this decision, observing that most manufacturers of bottled water were regional players and very few brands had an all-India presence.

Parle's Bisleri mineral water brand, the only national level player at that point of time, was expected to pose stiff competition to Eureka Forbes.

The fact that these developments came at a time when the partners in the Eureka Forbes joint venture, Forbes Gokak Ltd. (FGL) and Electrolux AB (Electrolux), were engaged in a bitter boardroom battle, added to the air of uncertainty surrounding the company.

The tiff had started in early 1999, when Electrolux announced its decision to walk out of the direct sales business worldover and, consequently, sell off its 40% stake in Eureka Forbes. Company observers stated that Eureka Forbes could find it difficult to succeed in the retail business without Electrolux's financial support and marketing expertise. The decisions to shift from direct selling to retailing and to enter the bottled water segment were being eyed with suspicion by analysts. Commenting on these decisions, analysts said that since Eureka Forbes was a relatively new player in the retail business and did not have much experience, it could have a tough future ahead.

Background Note
Fred Wardell, a well-known businessman of Detroit, Michigan, launched vacuum cleaners under the Eureka brand name in 1909. Eureka's vacuum cleaners were sleek, versatile and lightweight, while most of the vacuum cleaners manufactured those days were clumsy and difficult to use.

Within a few years, the company became well-known for its innovative product range. In 1913, Eureka launched vacuum cleaners in six different models and offered various add-ons for cleaning floors (bare/carpeted), walls, upholstery, and crevices. The company adopted the direct marketing route from the very beginning and its sales personnel delivered personalized services to customers.

As vacuum cleaners became increasingly popular in the early 1900s, Eureka employed around 5000 salesmen and opened over 400 branches to cater to growing customer demand. Within a decade, Eureka had established itself as the market leader in the Vacuum Cleaner industry.

The company acquired reputation for high quality products and excellent customer/dealer relations. In 1915, Eureka received the highest award for vacuum cleaners in those days, the 'Grand Prize,'by a jury of electrical experts at the San Francisco International Exposition.

Eureka Forbes - Starting From The Scratch
Eureka Forbes followed the globally 'tried and tested' direct selling route for marketing its products in India, thus becoming one of the first direct selling companies in India. Vacuum cleaners and water purifiers were rather new concepts for Indian consumers, who had till then followed only the traditional methods of cleaning and filtering.

Therefore, Eureka Forbes had to first establish the concept of vacuum cleaners and water purifiers in India before it could sell 'Eureka' as a brand. The company believed that its core strength was its people. It employed dynamic, highly motivated individuals, called 'Eurochamps,' who projected the image of 'The friendly man from Eureka Forbes.'

Thus, for the average Indian consumer, Eureka Forbes became synonymous with the smartly dressed salesman who came to their houses and cleaned up things in a jiffy or showed how air/water purifiers were indispensable. Eurochamps initially targeted the metros but soon began visiting smaller cities and towns also.

Future Prospects

Commenting on the decision to diversify into bottled water, company sources said that it was only to strengthen the core products by capitalizing on their brand image. Goklaney said, "In the water category, I will conduct activities which strengthen my core products. How I do that and what I do is a matter of strategy."

According to company sources, Eureka Forbes not only had the financial strength, but also a strong network of sales executives to push its new products into the market.

The company's decision to enter the retail business was primarily the result of its launch of 'Tornado' vacuum cleaners and 'Aquaflo' water purifiers in 1995.

Eureka Forbes had utilized the retail route for this range, mainly to cater to the industrial segment. Over the years, the retail business assumed greater significance and by 1999, around 5% of the company's sales came from the 2500-strong dealer network...

Source:
http://www.icmrindia.org/casestudies/catalogue/Marketing/MKTG022.htm

Questions:

1. You must have encountered a Eureka Forbes sales person at some point of time in your life. Have you noticed any significant difference between a Eureka Forbes sales person and a sales person of any other company coming at your doorstep? Give appropriate reasons for your answer.
2. What strategies should Eureka Forbes adopt to counter competition in the water purifying segment?

MARUTI Udyog LIMITED

Since 1985, Maruti Udyog Limited (MUL) has been the market leader in the passenger car industry in India. Its flagship product - M800 had the distinction of being the largest selling car model in India since its launch in December 1983.

Positioned as people's car, M800 ruled the Indian passenger car market and remained unchallenged ever since it occupied the top slot, five months after its introduction.

In March 2003, MUL sold 20,687 units of M800, the highest ever sales by any single model in a month. It was also the highest sales since M800 debuted, surpassing its previous monthly high of 18,735 units in August 1999.

For the first few months of 2004, M800 performed well, selling 15,301 units in January, 13,518 units in February and 15,540 in March. But gradually Alto, another MUL product, began eating into M800's share. Alto reported sales of 8,399 units, 8,324 and 9,011 units in January, February and March respectively.

In April, its sales increased to 9,350 units and in May 2004, Alto took over M800's position as the largest selling car with sale of 10,373 units, slightly over M800's sales of 10,016 units. Analysts felt that Alto had taken the top spot because of its price reduction in September 2003 by Rs. 23,000 followed by the launch of the non-AC Alto for Rs. 0.23 mn in the first week of April 2004. On reducing the gap between its bread and butter model M800 and its compact car Alto, MUL said it had "long term" plans for M800. Commenting on Alto's pricing strategy, Jagdish Khattar (Khattar), managing director of MUL, said, "The new price positioning of the Alto would cannibalize existing A1 segment product the M800 which is also considered an old model.

But, the cannibalization will remain within the Maruti family and the bigger numbers will help Maruti depreciate Alto faster. Net M800 sales may be less but we would be pushing more Alto and the more we sell the Alto the faster it will depreciate." Though industry analysts said this move would boost MUL's profits, they also expressed their views that MUL's long-term plan might be to discontinue M800 and replace the entry segment with Alto.

However, Khattar clarified that MUL's pricing strategy was not meant to replace M800 with Alto. He said, "Now, we have two cars in entry-level. Maruti 800 is still a dream of Indians, how can I replace it?"

Background Note
In its efforts to fulfill the growing demand for personal transport vehicles, the Government of India (GoI) established MUL in February 1981 through an Act of Parliament. It was incorporated to take over the assets of the erstwhile Maruti Limited set up in June 1971 and wound up by High Court order in 1978. In

October 1982, the GoI signed a joint venture agreement with Suzuki Motor Corporation (SMC) of Japan.

MUL received technology support from SMC. On the other hand, SMC got support from the Indian government, which helped it get import clearances for manufacturing equipment and obtain land for its factory.

At the time of its establishment, the objectives of MUL were:

• Modernization of the Indian automobile industry.

• Production of fuel-efficient vehicles to conserve scarce resources.

• Production of large number of motor vehicles, which was necessary for growth.

In an era when owning a car was a distant dream for a vast majority of Indians, MUL rolled out its first car, the M800. The company labeled it a people's car, with a 796cc 3-cylinder engine that delivered 39.5bhp at an affordable price of Rs. 65,000. The first vehicle was released for sale in December 1983. Initially, the car was criticized for its diminutive size, but it proved to be spacious enough to carry four adults.

The Indian passenger car market was divided into various segments and sub-segments on the basis of price, size (i.e. length of the model and its weight) and other factors (including engine capacity). MUL had a presence in all the segments and sub-segments.

The Pricing Strategy
Due to the fierce competition in the Indian passenger car industry, price emerged as an important factor affecting the purchasing decisions of customers. Since it had been in the industry for more than two decades, and as a market leader, MUL adopted aggressive pricing strategies.

The company had products at various price points. In the early 2000s, when the passenger car industry was witnessing stagnation, MUL slashed the prices of its various models, to revive the industry.

Promotion and Distribution
In the early 2000s, MUL also focused on promotion and distribution to face intense competition. The company devised various innovative promotional strategies. With interest rates declining from 12% to as low as 8% in automobile finance, MUL used financing as a major tool to drive up its car sales. The overall percentage of cars being financed through automobile loans increased from 65% in 1998 to over 85% in 2003

The Result

By 2004, the competition in the Indian passenger car industry had further intensified. However, MUL retained its leadership position mainly due to its aggressive pricing strategy. In December 2004, MUL reported an 18% rise in vehicle sales helped by a sharp increase in exports and rising demand in the domestic market.

Domestic sales increased by 11.4 percent amounting to 37,153 units, while exports jumped 78 percent to 6,675 units. After the price reductions and aggressive promotion, M800 and Alto sold in huge volumes in India.

Source:

http://www.icmrindia.org/casestudies/catalogue/Marketing/MKTG100.htm

Questions:

1. What have been the various reasons for Maruti's growth in market share?
2. Comment on the marketing mix of MUL?

MCDONALD'S

Introduction

It was early evening and one of the 25 McDonald's outlets in India was bustling with activity with hungry souls trooping in all the time. No matter what one ordered - a hot Maharaja Mac or an apple pie - the very best was served every time.

But did anyone ever wonder as to how this US giant managed the show so perfectly? The answer seemed to lie in a brilliantly articulated food chain, which extended from these outlets right up to farms all across India.

US-based fast food giant, McDonald's success in India had been built on four pillars: limited menu, fresh food, fast service and affordable price. Intense competition and demands for a wider menu, drive-through and sit-down meals - encouraged the fast food giant to customize product variety without hampering the efficacy of its supply chain.

Around the world (including India), approximately 85% of McDonald's restaurants were owned and operated by independent franchisees. Yet,

McDonald's was able to run the show seamlessly by outsourcing nine different ingredients used in making a burger from over 35 suppliers spread all over India through a massive value chain.

Between 1992 and 1996, when McDonald's opened its first outlet in India, it worked frenetically to put the perfect supply chain in place. It trained the local farmers to produce lettuces or potatoes to specifications and worked with a vendor to get the perfect cold chain in place. And explained to the suppliers precisely why only one particular size of peas was acceptable (if they were too large, they would pop out of the patty and get burnt).

These efforts paid off in the form of joint ventures between McDonald's India (a 100% wholly-owned subsidiary of McDonald's USA) and Hardcastle Restaurants Pvt. Ltd, (Mumbai) and Connaught Plaza Restaurant (New Delhi). Few companies appreciate the value of supply chain management and logistics as much as McDonald's does.

From its experience in other countries, McDonald's was aware that supply chain management was undoubtedly the most important factor for running its restaurants successfully. Amit Jatia, Managing Director, Hardcastle Restaurants Private Limited said, "A McDonald's restaurant is just the window of a much larger system comprising an extensive food-chain, running right up to the farms".

McDonald's worked on the supply chain management well ahead of its formal entry to India. "We spent seven years to develop the supply chain. The first McDonald's team came to India way back in 1989," said S. D. Saravanan (Saravanan), Product Manager, National Supply Chain, McDonald's India.

Background Note
McDonald's was started as a drive-in restaurant by two brothers, Richard and Maurice McDonald in California, US in the year 1937. The business, which was generating $200,000 per annum in the 1940s, got a further boost with the emergence of a revolutionary concept called 'self-service.'

The brothers used assembly line procedures in their kitchen for mass production. Prices were kept low. Speed, service and cleanliness became the critical success factors of the business. By mid-1950s, the restaurant's revenues had reached $350,000.

As word of their success spread, franchisees started showing interest. However, the franchising system failed because the McDonald brothers observed very transparent business practices. As a consequence, imitators copied their business practices and emerged as competitors. The franchisees also did not maintain the same standards of cleanliness, customer service and product uniformity.

At this point, Ray Kroc (Kroc), distributor for milkshake machines expressed interest in the business, and he finalized a deal with the McDonald brothers in 1954. He established a franchising company, the McDonald System Inc. and appointed franchisees. In 1961, he bought out the McDonald brothers' share for $2.7 million and changed the name of the company to McDonald's Corporation. In 1965, McDonald's went public.

In Search of Perfect Logistics - The Story of the Cold Chain
In 1996, when McDonald's entered India, it was looking for a distribution agent who would act as a hub for all its vendors. Mumbai-based Radhakrishna Foodland Private Limited (RFPL) was chosen for the job as it was already a distributor for its sister concern, Radhakrishna Hospitality Services, a catering unit supplying to offshore institutions. The iceberg lettuce from Ooty, mutton patties from Hyderabad and sesame seed buns from Punjab were all delivered to RFPL's distribution centre (cold storage) in its refrigerated vans. RFPL stored the products in controlled conditions in Mumbai and New Delhi and supplied them to McDonald's outlets on a daily basis.

By transporting the semi-finished products at a particular temperature, the cold chain ensured freshness and adequate moisture content of the food. The specially designed trucks maintained the temperature in the storage chamber throughout the journey. Drivers were instructed specifically not to switch off the chilling system to save electricity, even in the event of traffic jam.

Outsourcing at its Best
McDonald's sourced ingredients from all parts of India. (Refer Table I). The iceberg lettuce was specially developed for India using a new culture farming technique. This variety of lettuce was similar to the lettuce McDonald's used elsewhere in the world. To meet the demand consistently, McDonald's helped Trikaya Agriculture grow the lettuce throughout the year and even in rain-shadow areas. The crop was harvested between 45 days, depending on the climate. The crop was harvested early in the morning and immediately stored in vacuum pre-coolers installed at the farm. The pre-cooler brought down the temperature of the lettuce from 26° to 3°.

Source:
http://www.icmrindia.org/casestudies/catalogue/Operations/OPER001.htm

Questions:

1. Comment as to how have McDonald's unified the brand but then diversified the menu in Indian context?
2. Highlight the distribution strategy adopted by McDonald's?
3. Comment on the service marketing mix at McDonald's?

TUPPERWARE

Tupperware's Tryst with India

On April 27 2002, Christian Skroder (Skroder), vice president Tupperware company (Tupperware), felicitated about 900 star performers of Tupperware India, the Indian subsidiary of the $1.1 billion Tupperware company in the US. Skroder said that India was one of the largest markets for the company's products. The company had achieved a growth rate of 40% within four years of its entry in the Indian market.

In 1996, the company had a turnover of Rs.100 million, which according to analysts was an achievement in itself and in 2000, the company's turnover touched Rs.570 million.

Commented Rajan Chabba, deputy managing director of KSA Technopak, a retail consultancy, "At launch, Tupperware did a phenomenal job of creating a base in India and it has been growing ever since," According to analysts, Tupperware India performed better than most of the other foreign direct selling companies in India.

This was because it was focused on achieving its targets both in terms of sales as well as segments. The company was growth driven and pushed the direct selling method well. Tupperware India aimed at becoming the No 1 direct selling company in India, by 2004.

Background Note

In 1937, when Earl Silas Tupper worked in Dupont's[2] plastic division in Massachusetts, he transformed a piece of black polyethelyne slag, a waste product produced in crude oil refinement process, into a resilient, tough, non porous, non greasy and translucent substance.

He created many light weight, non breakable containers such as cups, plates, bowls etc, with this substance. Earl S. Tupper founded the Tupperware company in 1938. During the Second World War, the company concentrated on molding parts for Navy signal lamps and gas masks.

After the war, the company turned its attention to manufacturing plastic products for the growing consumer market. Its first consumer products were a bell shaped flexible container called the Bell Tumbler and the Wonderlier Bowl (a round bottomed bowl with a lid).

These products were superior to the traditional glass and crockery as they were unbreakable. Tupperware products were durable and were also easy to handle. They came in various attractive colours and shapes. At a time when Americans used glass and crockery to store and serve food items, Tupperware provided a more durable and reliable alternative.

Tupperware also designed the renowned air-tight, liquid proof lid in 1946. It was modeled on the inverted rim of a paint can. This lid prevented spillage and wiltage of the stored items and kept them fresh for a longer time. From its inception, Tupperware faced challenges in marketing its products. In 1946, though the Tupperware plastic products were introduced in hardware and department stores, they failed to generate demand.

It became clear that the company needed to educate the consumers about the quality and properties of the products. In the late 1940s, Brownie Wise, who was selling household products for Stanley Home Products was hired by Tupperware.

She gave Tupperware its unique "Party Plan" method of marketing. In 1948 Tupperware's first Home Party was conducted. Here, Tupperware products and their uses were demonstrated to consumers.

These demonstrations helped the company to explain to the customers, the quality, the usage and the reasons for higher cost of its products.

Brownie Wise was appointed the Vice President of the Tupperware company in 1951. She removed all Tupperware products from retail outlets and marketed them through the Party Plan method. The company concentrated on women as their prime sellers and consumers.

Tupperware in India
Tupperware entered India in November 1996. It started its operations from New

Delhi. It appointed 15 distributors in the first 12 months itself. It achieved this by directly recruiting candidates and training them, through a specially designed 14-week training program in Delhi and Mumbai. According to Pradeep Mathur (Mathur), the then managing director of Tupperware India, as the concept of direct selling was new to India, Tupperware had to sell both the direct selling concept and its 'Party Plan.'

The Tupperware Model

Tupperware, though a direct selling company, differed from other direct selling companies. It adopted a three- tier network structure which made operations easier for the company. Amway, another direct selling company, followed a model where the distributors were the centre of the model. They played multiple roles of retailers/distributors, sales agents, advertisers and promoters (word of mouth) for the suppliers' products.

Tupperware's marketing strategy was described by its three Ps- Product, Party plan and People. The Tupperware products carried a life time guarantee. Any damaged product (cracks or breaks) could be replaced by same/similar new Tupperware product from any place in the world. Mathur said, "Our product has been the corner stone of our success for many years."

Future Outlook

Tupperware was gaining fast recognition in the Indian market. Its 'Party Plan' worked well because it fitted in the urban and semi urban culture of 'kittie party. By 2002, the company expanded its operations to more than 35 cities in the country.

The company did not face any major competition from other plastic wares in India, as the quality of Tupperware goods was much better. However, Tupperware India competed with manufacturers of steel containers as Indian consumers used steel containers to store and carry food.

Source:

http://www.icmrindia.org/casestudies/catalogue/Marketing/MKTG086.htm

Questions:

1. Highlight on the unique aspects of the Tupperware model?
2. Highlight the factors that led to Tupperware's success in India?

ABS SALES

ABS Sales and Services Pvt. Limited is a DSA or a direct sales associate of ICICI Bank and it is into selling credit cards and personal loans to customers. The company has a sales team mainly comprising fresh graduates. Jatin and Manoj are members of the sales team who have quite different temperaments and attitudes to selling as a profession.

While both Jatin and Manoj are quite intelligent, it is Jatin who is more committed and persuasive by nature while Manoj is more of an escapist by nature when it comes to selling. Jatin is someone who considers the daily sales report quite seriously and feels it actually reflects his learning curve while Manoj manipulates a lot while filling up his daily sales reports. He is someone who tries make appointments over phone and more often than not tries to even sell over phone. He is creative that way but then alas! Its misplaced. Jatin makes lots of cold canvassing for prospecting purpose and hence he is never short of prospects.

At one point of time, Manoj had very little knowledge about the features of the products he was supposed to sell. Later, after interacting a lot with his colleagues, he was enlightened. Later on, when customer raised objections, he was found to take them head on and adopt the direct denial route which actually failed to help his cause.

A 6 month appraisal report showed Manoj far behind Jatin as far as target achievement was concerned. His boss, firmly asked Manoj to either pull up his socks or just leave the ship within the next two months.

Questions:

1. What type of salespersons were Jatin and Manoj?
2. What were the traits of good sales person that were missing in Manoj?
3. What were the shortcomings of Manoj in the context of prospecting?

4. Manoj adopted the direct denial method of objection handing which was found to backfire. What should have been the ideal way to handle customer objections?

JENKIN'S CORP.

Jenkin's Corp. is a MNC that has set its shop in India a year back. The company is basically a marketer of FMCGs like biscuits, cheese and various other confectionary items. The company after around 8months of its operations in India found that it was basically going nowhere. It had no positives to show. The head of the company's operations in India hired a business strategy consultant to identify the problem areas.

A careful study revealed that the problem lay with the work force of Jenkin's. They were least motivated, felt highly insecure and were least confident to carry on with their core tasks. First of all, the sales staff was not given adequate training on products and selling strategies. The company felt that selling cannot be taught; it can only be learnt. But then, suitable product knowledge was definitely an issue. The work force felt that the company was hardly interested in their respective career enhancements. Every month, three to four sales guys were asked to leave for the failure to achieve targets that were quite stiff compared to the market scenario. There was thus tremendous feeling of insecurity. Demotivation and insecurity were the two top factors for their consistent non-performance.

Questions:

1.What should Jenkin's do to motivate its staff?
2.Manpower is a greater resource than capital for a company. Do you agree? Give reasons to support your opinion.

BLACK & White Paper COMPANY

Black & White Paper Company is located in an agricultural belt about 300 kms from a metro city. The company is into writing and printing paper. It primary raw material is wheat straw. Last year, the company had a turnover of Rs. 134 crore on a volume of 45,000 tons of paper. While preparing the distribution plan for the current year, the top management was concerned with the following distribution issue that they want you as a student of management to resolve:

The major is that of distribution of finished goods. The paper industry is dominated by selling agents who bring the manufacturer like Black & White and the buyer like printing/publishing companies, and note book makers, together. They make a commission of about 2 per cent on all transactions. Some of the other problem areas:

- Black & White depends on about 110 agents to canvass business for it from the users
- The company sells about 23% of its paper directly to some government organizations
- The agent arranges for the buyer to pay the company for its produce by advance demand draft. It is expected that the agent provides the credit support to the buyer
- Agents are not exclusive for Black & White and work for other paper mills also and normally play the mills against each other. They have a grip on the business and are reluctant to put the mill directly in touch with the buyers
- There is always an uncertainty on the orders and the price, which would be obtained on the orders – the company cannot plan its profits properly nor offer the best service to the end users so that they always ask for Black & White.

Questions:

1. How can you help Black & White become less dependant on the selling agents and plan its sales and profitability better?
2. How can they plan their customer service efforts?

KOTAK FINANCE

Vishal was a sales representative for Kotak Finance. He was involved in selling Kotak's receivable collection services largely through cold calls. He randomly picked a building or office, went in and started chatting with secretaries. Before it was too long, these deceptively high conversations provided him with valuable names and information, and made his call a lot less cold.

Vishal on an average made thirty cold calls and four presentations per day. He has been a salesperson for fifteen years, and estimates that he has made over 15,000 cold calls during his career. His secrets to successful cold calling include thinking fast and never assuming the person he is talking to is not a decision maker.

In contrast to Kotak, prospecting at brokerage firm, Indus Finance made used of nonrandom and streamline approach. It operated on various job levels responsible for different parts of the prospecting process. About forty lower wage telemarketers had the sole responsibility to make unsolicited first contacts with potential customers. If telemarketers found the callers were interested, they transferred potential to other employees, called a 'qualifier'. Qualifier evaluated the prospect's investment objectives, willingness to accept following calls and financial ability. Telemarketers, who made initial contacts, reached hordes of people. In one four- day period the callers contacted 18,004 prospects and opened forty accounts.

Many industries criticized for leadgeneratio tactics such as massive telemarketing efforts to make sure that consumers are protected; government implemented certain limits on telephone and fax selling. The federal communications commission currently maintains a list of people who do not want to receive telemarketing calls, and companies are fined if they violate the wishes of those on the list. Auto dialing is being critically reviewed, and legislation 0 ban auto dialing to hospitals and other institutions that need: open limes in case of emergencies have before the government. Some rule makers are publishing to ban unsolicited sales calls in any cases where the callee has to foot the cost of the call (cellular phones, for instance); others want to ban all calls to homes.

There are those who say that cold calling is dead. Cold calls are often unpopular; however, they can also be quite effective if the benefit to the customer is legitimate and the salesperson sincere. At Kotak Finance, cold calling is based on dynamic personal selling. Organized technology is Indus Finance focus. For both companies, cold calling is, at least for the time being, very much alive.

Questions:

1. Compare and contrast cold calling at Kotak Finance and Indus Finance. Do they follow the same approach while qualifying the potential customers?

2. How can a salesperson find out whether or not a prospect has the financial resources to buy? What other factors should be considered when' qualifying a prospect?

3. Organizations prefer telemarketing or cold-calls with an objective to make a sales deal. Explain the sales objectives assuming that your organization has adopted either one of these approaches.

Source: Sales & Distribution Management, M.V. Kulkarni

NARANE ESTATES

Real estate sellers often face Objection from potential homebuyers who are not sure that they cannot afford the house they want. To help to solve .is problem the sales staff at Narane Estates, has been provided with computers to respond to such objections.

After a salesperson plugs in information about a prospect income, savings, and debt situation, specially designed software determines whether the prospect can handle a mortgage. The prospect is provided with the information that includes" in addition to data on the ability to afford a home, rent or buy comparisons and available options for all the homes the prospect is interested in. Once the prospects know a new home is affordable, continuity with the sales process is usually much easier.

Another advantage of the computers is their speed. Without the computers, salespersons had to perform calculations by hand, and they were often distracted from the sale itself. Equipped with computers, I salespeople are able to make a more seamless presentation.

Narane's computers are no substitutes for good personal selling, but they are very useful to agents faced with the "I don't know if I can afford it" objection. With the computers, salespersons are able to respond to this objection quickly and efficiently, and greatly increase their chances of getting to the next phase of selling process-the close.

Questions:

1. How do the advance selling equipments like e-computers help the salespersons in attracting the potential customers?
2. Salespersons face sales objection in the processes of selling. As a sales manager what basic rules and method do you suggest to handle the objections?
3. Explain the various types of sales objectives that salesperson is likely to face. In case of Narane, what type of objection do its salespersons face?
4. With the computers, salespersons are able to respond to the objections quickly and greatly increase their chances of getting to the next phase of selling process-the close. What do you mean by close and when can a salesperson close?

Source: Sales & Distribution Management, M.V. Kulkarni

SELLING the Rocket Singh WAY!

On December 11th 2009, *Rocket Singh: Salesman of the Year*, a movie made under the Yash Raj Films (YRF) banner was released across the country. The movie directed by Shimit Amin and starring Ranbir Kapoor offered insights on effective tools and techniques of sales management. What was great about the movie was that we audiences were introduced to the secrets of successful and sustainable selling in an extremely entertaining and convincing manner without being too preachy.

Rocket Singh: Salesman of the Year proved to be one of the myriad movies over the years that successfully mirrored the aspects, attitudes and aspirations of the contemporary Indian society. Indian cinema has often featured various aspects, issues, taboos and personalities on celluloid. From Dadasaheb Phalke to Farhan Akhtar, every decade of Indian cinema witnessed filmmakers who in their own way contributed to raising and portraying various socially relevant issues. The pathos of partition, the problems of a newly independent nation, the turbulence of the 1970s, the rise in global terrorism, the wars fought by India with its neighboring nations, the business of prostitution, AIDS awareness were some of the various topics that had been the major subjects of several movies.

However since the early 2000s, we came across few movies that had loads of content relevant to potential as well as practicing management executives. Movies like *Lagaan, Corporate* and *Chak De! India* were some that deserved a special mention in the said context. While the plots of movies like *Lagaan* and *Chak De! India* had indirect relevance to various management principles and practices, the recently released movie *Rocket Singh: Salesman of the Year* delved directly into a particular subject domain of management and that was Sales management apart from offering certain general management insights.

The *Rocket Singh* Plot
Rocket Singh: Salesman of the Year was the story of Harpreet Singh Bedi who was extremely poor in academics and somehow just managed to pass his graduation. Ranbir Kapoor played the role of Harpreet in the movie. Harpreet was inducted as a trainee at AYS Computers, a company that was into the sales and services of computers. The sales manager of the company was against the induction but upon the insistence of the company's top boss, Harpreet was offered the job. While being offered buddy training by the sales manager, Harpreet observed few things that were not quite to his liking like offering bribes to seek a customer's appointment. Few days later, when Harpreet was sent on a sales call, the client asked for bribe which Harpreet flatly refused and further lodged a formal complaint with his company. The top boss of the company, Mr. Puri reacted furiously to this and asked Harpreet to just complete his training period and leave the company after that. He warned him from creating any further 'ruckus' (doing anything that was not the norm in the company) in the company. Soon Harpreet turned into a laughing stock for his colleagues. He was mocked at

every now and then by everyone at the office. Unable to bear the humiliation on a regular basis, Harpreet thought of an idea. An idea of opening his own business of computer sales and service that would religiously work for client's cause and that would not perform any unethical business practice. He coined his potential company's name as Rocket Sales Corporation.

Harpreet was meticulous in scouting for the right sort of people at AYS Computers who can become partners in his venture. First he persuaded the receptionist of the company to join him since he was well aware of her potential as a telecaller. Next he had the person who looked after the services aspect followed by an office boy who used to deliver tea and at times offer a helping hand for assembling computers. Finally Harpreet had the company's Sales Manager's consent to join his venture. Each and every person worked as a partner in the venture and had equal stakes in it. The business philosophy of Rocket Sales Corporation was distinctly different from AYS Computers. Its policies were more customer- friendly and ethical due to which it appealed to customers in no time and scored an ace over AYS Computers. Mr. Puri was perplexed at the development and tried hard to find out the people who were behind Rocket Sales Corporation and soon he found out that the company comprised of some of his own employees who were using the company's infrastructure to solicit and service clients. He dismissed all his employees who were attached with Rocket Sales Corporation including Harpreet and went for a hostile takeover of Rocket Sales Corporation. Mr.Puri's company was branded as AYS Rocket Sales Corp after the acquisition. His existing staff members were found to cater to both AYS as well as Rocket Sales Corporation clients. Soon, there was growing dissatisfaction among the clients who found sales and service policies of AYS Rocket Sales Corp quite unfriendly and unethical. The company started loosing clients drastically. Mr. Puri finally understood that just by acquiring the brand of Rocket Sales Corporation, he was no way benefitted. He was required to provide the service quality that Harpreet and his small team used to commit and provide to customers. He understood that any business was about people working for it and their skills and any business was about effective inter-personal interaction without which sustainability of a business would be a big question.

Mr. Puri finally met Harpreet at a retail outlet where Harpreet was working as a customer sales associate. He accepted his defeat stating he was wrong in analyzing the way any business worked in the 21st century. He was wrong in under estimating his customers and going about offering bribes to them to retain them. He gave back the document that Harpeet had earlier signed when Mr. Puri acquired Rocket Sales Corporation stating that Rocket Sales Corporation was Harpeet's from then on. The final scene of the movie featured Harpreet working in his company along with his previous partners; his lady love and his grandfather all working as partners looking after different aspects of the company.

Sales Management on Celluloid

The books on sales and marketing management have often mentioned that there has been a transformation from the seller's to the buyer's market over the years. Various write ups in the domain of consumer behavior and marketing have mentioned today's customer as the king meaning that companies of today need to go by what the customer beliefs and wants and not as per their own whims and fancies. Companies of today need to make a shift from product-oriented to service-oriented mentality. They need to think of creating strong differentiation for their goods or services so that they appeal to customers, gain revenues and earn profits in due course of time. The business world has experienced a paradigm shift as far as orientations of companies across various industries are concerned. Companies have understood and adopted the marketing concept over the selling concept to further their profits in today's competitive scenario.

Rocket Singh: Salesman of the Year as a movie stressed on all the above aspects and much more. Just as in movies like *Lagaan* and *Chak De! India*, *Rocket Singh: Salesman of the Year* portrayed some basic leadership qualities through the character of Harpreet Singh Bedi. The basic ingredient of a leader to spot talents for his team and make each team member feel equally significant to the team's cause was one aspect that got reflected. Each of his four team members were selected by Harpreet as part of his team because of certain expertise they had acquired as employees of AYS Computers. Each team member was offered equal partnership stake so that there was no sort of inequality and no one felt any sort of injustice being done to him or her. This was found to boost the overall morale of the unit. A leader should take the entire responsibility when anything goes wrong and should ensure to shield his team members and that's exactly what Harpreet did when Mr. Puri found out the origin of Rocket Sales Corporation and its members. He accepted the hostile take over of his company by Mr. Puri without any resistance because that was the only way to avoid any further harm happening to his unit members.

There are two variants of selling viz. transactional selling and relationship selling. At one point time, transactional selling was omnipresent but over the years there has been significant evolution in the selling approach and now it is relationship selling that rules the roost. In *Rocket Singh: Salesman of the Year*, we audiences got to experience both forms of selling. When Harpreet turned up for an interview at AYS Computers, the receptionist made a mention about salesmen making the sale but not bothering to take the customer feedback about the product's performance. That selling attitude is transactional selling where the relationship between the seller and the customer ends with the salesperson making the sale. The salesperson in this context is least interested to attend to customer problems after the sale. When Harpreet formed Rocket Sales Corporation, the selling approach that he adopted was relationship selling. First and foremost he was not the kind of salesperson who was always at pushing products at the customer thinking about his own interests. Rather he tried to analyze the requirements of the customer and understand the best solution possible for the person. This approach in sales management is termed as SPIN approach to relationship selling where SPIN is the acronym for Situation, Problem, Implication and Need Pay off.

An effective sales person is one who tries to analyze the present situation of the customer and what kind of problems is the customer facing due to the said situation. He needs to understand the implications of the problem for the customer and then offer a product that will be a solution to the problem. Harpreet's very first customer was a lady who was trying to set up a business with meager budget. She could not afford to pay high prices for the infrastructure required for her business, one of which was computers. Harpreet after scouting the market based on the affordability factor of his customer designed a solution that was the best available within the limits of the budget.

In the movie, we found AYS Computers to be a recognized brand and profitable company in its industry but then we also understood that the profits earned by the company was through higher sales volume that was achieved unethically in most cases. Customers were either cheated or they were bribed to claim orders. There was hardly any sort of focus on customer needs. In other words the company followed the selling concept in achieving its profits that actually proved to be unsustainable in the long run. Within a short span of time, Rocket Sales Corporation was found to taste profits in its business and that came through customer satisfaction. Customer was the focal point of his business and an integrated marketing approach was used to conduct the business. Harpreet created significant, relevant and tangible differentiation for his business in terms of annual service maintenance charges and through flexible timings of offering service to customers. Customers acknowledged and appreciated the differentiation and responded positively which offered greater business sustainability. Harpreet's concept of running the business is called the marketing concept.

Time management is an important ingredient of sales management. Sales executives need to acknowledge the importance of time and organize their work in such a way that wastage of time is minimized. In other words time available is utilized to the optimum level. When Harpreet and his team members who were all employees of AYS Computers was in a spot of bother as how to manage their jobs as well as their business, Harpreet came up with an unique idea that was especially helpful for the person who was in charge of computer servicing and assembling and that was to do the needful after the end of office hours from the premises of AYS Computers. The person was thus able to manage both his job as well as his business interests and maximum utilization of time was possible.

Sales territories and management of sales territories is an important aspect of sales management that got highlighted when Harpreet was newly recruited at AYS Computers. His senior colleagues made it clear that under no circumstances he should approach any client who belongs to their territories. Poaching of clients by employees of same company is a common occurrence which is an unethical practice. Often in order to meet their targets, sales executives enter the territories of their colleagues and intentionally approach their clients to sell their products.

Rocket Singh: Salesman of the Year is a testimony to the innovative approach that filmmakers are implementing while making movies. Movies in India have come a long way from being pure song and dance routines along with unconvincing plots to being socially relevant and believable. Education through entertainment can be the best possible way of seeking knowledge and *Rocket Singh: Salesman of the Year* does provide that.

ABOUT the AUTHOR

Kisholoy Roy is an Accredited Management Teacher from India who is a prolific writer and has written several books, case studies, articles and research papers in the domain of marketing. He is presently pursuing his doctorate in management from Indian School of Mines, Dhanbad in the area of Celebrity endorsements and Product placements.

He has over 100 publications to his name and believes that learning can be fun provided there is a good teacher who knows inside out of a subject and then there are students who are self disciplined with strong focus and determination.

www.ingramcontent.com/pod-product-compliance
Lightning Source LLC
Chambersburg PA
CBHW060407190526
45169CB00002B/791